FORKED TONGUES

The editor and publisher gratefully acknowledge the support of the following institutions in the publication of this volume:

The Spanish Ministerio de Economía y Competitividad, which has funded the research project on contemporary Irish and Galician women writers FFI2009-08475/FILO.

The Asociación de Escritores en Lingua Galega (AELG) for their financial support to the translators of Galician poetry in this anthology and for their long-standing endorsement of our research.

The Ramon Llull Institute for the grant for the translation of the poems by Vinyet Panyella, Susanna Rafart, Gemma Gorga and Mireia Calafell, translated from Catalan into English, by Michael O'Loughlin, Paula Meehan, Keith Payne, Theo Dorgan and the supervisor of the Catalan section, Dr Diana Cullell.

Forked Tongues

Galician, Basque and Catalan Women's Poetry in Translations by Irish Writers

Edited by

Manuela Palacios

Shearsman Books

First published in in the United Kingdom in 2012 by
Shearsman Books Ltd
50 Westons Hill Drive
Emersons Green
BRISTOL
BS16 7DF

Shearsman Books Ltd Registered Office
30–31 St. James Place, Mangotsfield, Bristol BS16 9JB
(this address not for correspondence)

www.shearsman.com

ISBN 978-1-84861-241-9
First Edition

Introduction © Manuela Palacios González, 2012.
All rights reserved.

The translations printed here are copyright © 2012 by:
Maurice Harmon (poems by Pilar Pallarés), Lorna Shaughnessy (Chus Pato),
Anne Le Marquand Hartigan (Lupe Gómez Arto),
Máighréad Medbh (Yolanda Castaño), Mary O'Donnell (María do Cebreiro),
Celia de Fréine (Itxaro Borda), Catherine Phil MacCarthy (Miren Agur
Meabe), Susan Connolly (Castillo Suárez), Paddy Bushe (Leire Bilbao),
Michael O'Loughlin (Vinyet Panyella), Paula Meehan (Susanna Rafart),
Keith Payne (Gemma Gorga), Theo Dorgan (Mireia Calafell).

Cover photograph copyright © Arturo Casas, 2012;
landscape art copyright © José Crespí Rodríguez, 2009.

All of the original-language texts contained in this volume
are copyright © by their individual authors.

We are grateful to the original publishers for permission to reprint such texts
as have been published previously, and also for their permission to publish the
translations in this volume. Full details of the source volumes and
permissions granted may be found on pp.183–184.

Contents

Introduction by Manuela Palacios — 7

Galician Poets

Pilar Pallarés	(Maurice Harmon)	23
Chus Pato	(Lorna Shaughnessy)	33
Lupe Gómez Arto	(Anne Le Marquand Hartigan)	43
Yolanda Castaño	(Máighréad Medbh)	55
María do Cebreiro	(Mary O'Donnell)	65

Basque Poets

Itxaro Borda	(Celia de Fréine)	77
Miren Agur Meabe	(Catherine Phil MacCarthy)	91
Castillo Suárez	(Susan Connolly)	103
Leire Bilbao	(Paddy Bushe)	113

Catalan Poets

Vinyet Panyella	(Michael O'Loughlin)	125
Susanna Rafart	(Paula Meehan)	137
Gemma Gorga	(Keith Payne)	151
Mireia Calafell	(Theo Dorgan)	161

Notes — 170
Authors and Translators — 171
Sources and Permissions — 183

I speak with the forked tongue of colony
>	Eavan Boland, *The Lost Land*

Tides came and went
with me listening
to those whispering
was it possible to speak
with a forked tongue   to sing
with a tongue not soaked in milk?
>	Marilar Aleixandre, *Catalogue of Poisons*

Women Poets in Translation. An Introduction

The trope of the forked tongue hovers over this bilingual collection of poetry. It is primarily intended to suggest the relationship between the source and the target languages—between the vernacular tongues of Galicia, the Basque Country, and Catalonia on the one hand and English as a *lingua franca* on the other. But the notion of the forked tongue arises also of the bilingual condition both of the writers and of the communities involved in this anthology. Galicia, the Basque country and Catalonia each have two official languages, and so has Ireland. Their writers' mutual understanding in this respect, alongside these communities' sundry political and cultural bonds, lie as the main motivations for the present selection of writers. In these four communities, the vernacular tongue coexists with another powerful language—Spanish or English—which has spread throughout centuries over many other nations. It is to this postcolonial condition that the Irish poet Eavan Boland alludes when she says: "I speak with the forked tongue of colony." The Madrid-born poet Marilar Aleixandre, on her part, delves into the choice of Galician as her literary language, though it was not her mother tongue: "to sing / with a tongue not soaked in milk." Historical and political circumstances have made of Galician, Basque and Catalan *minoritized* vernaculars, a phenomenon which justifies the necessity of positive action towards their visibilization and dissemination, such as the one this anthology aspires to facilitate by including the original texts.

Translation also seems to be an apt trope for intercultural relationships. "The common language of Europe is translation," affirms the Italian philosopher Giacomo Marramao in a statement that acknowledges cultural diversity and difference in the face of homogenization. The meeting point of the languages spoken in Europe—with or without a state, official or not, vernaculars or foreign languages imported by immigrant groups—is translation because, otherwise, there is no genuine encounter but submission. Translation is a performative act by which the Other is acknowledged. It is also a new opportunity to renegotiate our cultural bonds on fairer terms. The encounter favoured by translation necessarily entails some conflict too, as it is rarely a meeting of equals. The enormous gap between a world language such as English and the vernaculars in this anthology clearly illustrates this conflict, but the international language is also putting its extraordinary power of dissemination at the service of the more geographically-restricted vernacular tongues. A bilingual edition like this one circumvents the risk of the bear hug, which would consist in allowing the dissemination of vernacular literatures through monolingual translation but would conceal their languages, thereby adding to their further suppression.

There has been some debate about whether poets should translate other poets. The Mexican writer Octavio Paz suggests that the creative impulse in literary writers who engage in translation might make their texts stray too far from the original version. Along a similar line, Madeleine Stratford has warned about those renderings which bring into focus the poet/translator's interventions, while leaving the writer of the source text in an excessively subdued light, and therefore result in the translator's promotion at the expense of a distorted diffusion of the original author. On the opposite side of the debate and contrary to dismissals that deem writers' engagement in translation work as amateurish, the Galician writer and academic María do Cebreiro Rábade Villar vindicates the role of creative writers' translations, which often result from writers' affinities and mutual admiration, as a necessary counterbalance to the programming and economic interests of the literary market.

The English versions in *Forked Tongues* do not take the original poems as a mere source of inspiration for the elaboration of substantially different texts. Each language has, no doubt, its own rhythm and musicality; its words often have divergent histories and trigger different associations; its literary themes have received distinct elaborations in each literary tradition. For all these reasons, the English versions are necessarily new creations, but they are also co-creations which do not hide their relationship with the source poems: they do not cancel or ignore them, but are attentive and incorporate their concerns and motifs. The English poems thus establish with the source texts an imaginative dialogue in a common search for beauty and authenticity, "contending only for the glory of the language," as Osip Mandelstam has suggested in his discussion of Russian translations (in McGuckian and Ní Dhomhnaill). The majority of the Irish poets in this anthology had previous experience in the translation of literature from the community they engage with here, especially in the case of Galician and Catalan writing. In addition to their background in the source culture, most Irish poets have received the literal translations and, when necessary, literary and linguistic supervision from three specialists in the vernaculars represented here: Dr. Kirsty Hooper for Galician poetry, Dr. Juan Arana for Basque poetry and Dr. Diana Cullell for Catalan poetry, the three of them from the University of Liverpool. I would like to express my immense gratitude for the enthusiasm and diligence in their collaboration with this project. *Forked Tongues* is, therefore, a communal, collaborative effort that substantiates the plurality of actors who intervene in the production and dissemination of poetry.

§

The unprecedented upsurge of women writers since the nineteen eighties in the four communities represented in this anthology has been one of the most decisive motors of change in their literary systems. One cannot deny the importance, for this phenomenon, of the long struggle of the feminist movement since the early twentieth century and, in particular, that of the pivotal second wave in the nineteen seventies. Women's generalized access to secondary education, and for a substantial number of them to university degrees, has facilitated the broad and solid cultural background needed to become a writer. The gradual, though still incomplete, liberation of women from time-consuming domestic tasks and the commitments of large families has also been a necessary condition in the advance of women writers. *Forked Tongues* wishes to recognize these women's contribution to the normalization and consolidation of their respective literary systems. Male writers should do well to involve themselves in this struggle for the visibility of their female counterparts and this is the reason why, while the Galician, Basque and Catalan poets in this anthology are all women, a number of male poets have been included among the Irish translators.

The rise of women writers in Spain was in part favoured by the instability of political and cultural institutions after General Franco's death in 1975. Times of change may become appropriate occasions for emergent groups to elbow their way into literary centres. Galicia, the Basque Country and Catalonia are recognized as *historical nationalities* in the Spanish Constitution (1978) on account of their respective Statutes of Autonomy before the Spanish Civil War (1936–1939). With the advent of democracy after Franco's demise, new Statutes of Autonomy were passed in Catalonia (1979 and 2006), the Basque Country (1979) and Galicia (1981) which have committed their governments to protect and promote their vernacular languages and cultures. The emergence of women writers in the nineteen eighties, then, coincided with a period of nationalist self-affirmation, although their respective struggles have not always been encompassed with equity. Helena González Fernández has actually referred to the identity oxymoron woman/nation provoked by the subordination of women's interests to the *totalizing umbrella* of the national cause.

Galician Poetry

In the decade of the nineteen nineties, almost one hundred poets published their first individual poetry collection in Galician (Letras de Cal Editorial Board). The spectacular rise in the number of women poets generated the perception of a decade dominated by an alleged *feminine aesthetics*, with the subsequent risk of homogenizing both the writers and their work. A number of critics, however, have acknowledged women writers' key role in the renovation of the Galician literary system: "After the decline of socio-realism in the 1970s, poetic innovation in Galicia has come more steadily from women than men" (Rodríguez García). Except for Pilar Pallarés, whose first collection appeared in 1980, the rest of the Galician poets in *Forked Tongues* published their first book of verse in the nineties. This decade has been characterized by, among other features, women's repossession of the female body in literary tradition, the elegiac representation of the rural world, the shift of attention to urban, everyday life, the interrogation of the *fatherland* and other hegemonic discourses, and the recourse to conversational and casual linguistic registers (Nogueira). These general features match some, but by no means all, of the poetic explorations represented in this anthology.

Although **Pilar Pallarés** (1957) has vindicated the roots of her writing in social poetry and has been rather vocal about her left-wing nationalist convictions, her poetry usually turns inwards to explore the disputes of the self with the conditions of existence. In her view, "one writes about lack, about what has been lost, denied or forbidden" (in Cambeiro López). Her philological training—a common trait in many of the poets in this anthology—has provided her both with models from a broad range of national and international writers and with the necessary linguistic skills in a language, such as Galician, which has undergone a profound process of normalization and normativization in the last three decades. In her poetry, Pallarés acknowledges the literary influence of a number of women writers who have also left a deep imprint in the work of the other poets in this collection: Emily Dickinson, Virginia Woolf,

Djuna Barnes, Sylvia Plath, Alfonsina Storni, Alejandra Pizarnik, Clarice Lispector... Like their writing, the poems Pallarés has selected for the present anthology reflect on "transience and the process of decay and regeneration, on the art of life of our animal being, which we tend to ignore, on symbolic expression and the search for the sharpened word, the broken, thinned and necessary word" (in Casas 2003). Maurice Harmon, also a translator of the Galician poet Ana Romaní, masterfully renders the elegance and poise of Pallarés' phrasing.

The next poet in the Galician section—poets are ordered following the date of publication of their first book of poems—**Chus Pato** (1955), published her first collection in 1991 but it was her seventh book *m-Talá*, in 2000, that was recognized as a landmark of poetic renewal in Galicia due to its interrogation of literary representation and genre boundaries, its dramatization of speaking voices, its challenge to the conventions of language and logic, and its sustained dialogue with philosophy, history and literary tradition. Pato's poetry has delved into the themes of exploitation, dispossession, totalitarianism and the possibilities of emancipation. Her writing has been defined as: "torn poetry that fragments and breaks itself up, that interrupts and disperses itself, that goes from one thought to another, from one place to another, from one time to another in an infinitesimal space" (Raña). Pato has selected for this anthology several unpublished poems which illustrate the paths of experimentation she is currently exploring. She takes delight in visual forms, textures, colours, reflections and lines that fuse art and nature. Although she has on some occasion commented that her poetry is not musical, here she includes verse in which visual rhythm goes hand in hand with musical rhythm, and Lorna Shaughnessy, who also translated Pato in the past, deftly conveys the cadences of these Galician poems. In line with her previous writing, Pato continues to inquire into those liminal and porous spaces between melody and meaning, art and life, language and voice, because she firmly believes that "a poem [is] that writing which tries to capture what lies outside a language's enclosure" (in Casas 2011).

The poems by **Lupe Gómez Arto** (1972) in *Forked Tongues* were chosen in a collaborative way by the author and me. Gómez wanted to include some texts from her collection *Diálogos imposíbeis* [Impossible Dialogues] (2010) and allowed me to choose them, while I was also interested in her *début* collection, *Pornografía* [Pornography](1995), from which she chose its first poem and I selected her highly influential and widely quoted poem "Enfoque teórico" ([Theoretical Focus], "A Clinical

Stare" in Anne Hartigan's translation). In the poems from her 1995 collection, the poet challenges the ideal of feminine beauty and deals with women's repossession of their bodies, while also examining the tensions between woman and nation. The texts from her 2010 collection constitute a reflection on the craft of writing, the writer's literary complicities and the reciprocal nourishment of the various artistic manifestations, with special emphasis on the intersections of poetry with cinema and theatre. The apparent *naïveté* of her style, her vindication of fantasy and her humorous stance feel like a breath of fresh air which is perfectly matched by Anne Le Marquand Hartigan's spontaneous and irreverent tone. Lupe Gómez Arto has been identified as a provocative libertarian because of her sexually explicit language, which prudish readers consider to be in bad taste, and she is indeed convinced that art should interrogate our preconceptions (Alonso). As one of her poetic voices claims in *Azul e estranxeira* [Blue and Foreign] (2005): "I am sitting / on the stairway / to the plane. / I like this place, / I'm comfortable. / In the structure / of questions. / In circular poetry."

In her poetry, **Yolanda Castaño** (1977) scrutinizes the individual as a site of conflicting discourses—consumerist and disinterested, cosmopolitan and nationalist, *fashionista* and feminist, self-centred and cooperative, pragmatic and idealist, fraudulent and authentic, etc. Her writing pitilessly exposes our contradictions, our ineffectual quests and the lies we tell ourselves, and she does so by fragmenting and decentring the subject, by splitting the speaking voice from the construct of her poetic self, as in her cherished trope of the ventriloquist. Her relish for the masks we wear in our various subject positions is in line with her empowering public performances, which is the reason why I thought of Máighréad Medbh, also a remarkable performance poet, as her best possible translator. The poems Castaño has selected for this anthology illustrate her penchant for introspection and the proliferation of fictional selves, her anxiety about social bargaining and her exposure of the disconcerting effects of physical beauty in those moralistic and intellectual coteries which would rather transcend it. Máighréad Medbh bestows upon the English readers a sophisticated version of Castaño's transgressive syntax, unconventional punctuation and tantalizing imagery.

In her conversation with the Welsh poet Menna Elfyn, **María do Cebreiro** (1976) reflects, in a way that is also relevant for *Forked Tongues*, on the relationship between a *minoritized* language such as Galician and a hegemonic one such as English: "I believe in an idea of language that is constantly contaminated by other languages, voices, sounds. As of late I am using titles in English (also French and Spanish, but particularly English, as it's really perceived as the hegemonic language *par excellence*) in my poems in Galician. I am very much drawn to the visual force of that clash between a hegemonic language and a language such as Galician, only spoken in that tiny corner in Spain" (*Poetry Wales*). The poet thus turns a possible source of conflict, due to the imbalance of power between these languages, into an effective device of defamiliarization and a poetic trope of fertile miscegenation. Mary O'Donnell, who first conceived this project of Irish writers translating Galician poets for the anthology *To the Winds Our Sails*—a collection that has served as a guide for the present one—is then the most congenial translator of María do Cebreiro's ongoing interrogation of the limits of language, literary conventions and the preconceptions of literary criticism.

Basque Poetry

The Basque critic Jon Kortazar has suggested that it was only after General Franco's death that Basque literature became a literary system. As in Galicia, the Statute of Autonomy of the Basque Country (1979) encouraged the promotion of the vernacular language and facilitated spaces for the publication and criticism of Basque-language literature, with the concomitant upsurge of writers. As late as 1999, Kortazar remarked, however, that there remained an obstacle to be removed: the dearth in translations of Basque literature into foreign languages. Although important efforts have been made in this respect since then, the translation of women-authored poetry is still scarce and this anthology constitutes a step towards the dissemination of Basque-language women poets.

As in other stateless nations struggling for recognition, Basque women poets have been expected to adapt their writing to national *grand narratives* and identitary signs. In line with this, Tere Irastorza has commented on literary expectations in the nineteen eighties: "the general tendency in Basque literature at that time was to the attachment to our own language, which impeded the development of anything connected with everyday life" (in Fernández Iglesias). Some of the features to be found in these women writers are: the contestation of dominant discourses, whether moral, nationalist or patriarchal; the importance of keeping memory alive; the concern with what has been silenced; the search for new language and literary codes that allow us to apprehend reality differently; the repossession of women's body and sexual desire and the exploration of private, domestic experience as a poetic *topos* (Fernández Iglesias).

If Galicia has traditionally been seen as sharing Celtic roots with Ireland, the connections between the Basque Country and Ireland that we most often come across in the media are related to the struggle for national independence and the peace process (Rodríguez Bornaetxea). With this anthology, writers of both nationalities explore other kinds of collaboration and other imaginaries that do not reduce Ireland and the Basque Country to political violence. I have selected poets from two different generations: two who grew up and started writing in a very hostile social and cultural context before 1979 and two who formed themselves as writers after the Basque Statute of Autonomy was passed. The first poet, **Itxaro Borda** (1959), is from *Iparralde*—the Northern Basque Country in the south-west of France. With a degree in History, she is a poet and a fiction writer who has been rather vocal in her contestation of national identity as dictated by some gurus of nationalism. Of her own writing, she has said: "My verse is direct. It sometimes hurts like a blow. It is, most often, like a melancholic caress. It can always be sung, whether free or rhymed verse. It usually has the rhythm of a walk, as if poetic thought were infused with endomorphins" (in Ediciones La Palma). The poems she has selected for this collection either rewrite Basque literary tradition and, in particular, the role it has allocated to women—in this respect, no one could be a better match than her translator Celia de Fréine—or initiates a dialogue with other inspiring women artists, from the Catalan poet Maria-Mercè Marçal to the feminist theorist Judith Butler or *the queen of psychedelic soul*, Janis Joplin.

A number of poems by **Miren Agur Meabe** (1962) have already appeared in English translation in *Six Basque Poets* (Olaziregi). Her poetry has been defined as: "intense and effective, written from the daily context of a female subject who is totally conscious of her body and desire" (Fernández Iglesias). For *Forked Tongues*, she has chosen poems which illustrate this still much-needed woman-centred focus: a middle-aged woman's renunciations and defeats, her memories of the earliest betrayals and humiliations, and her ironic and down-to-earth surrender to the pleasures of the body. Like María do Cebreiro, Meabe reflects on the media's handling of human suffering as a spectacle and on the writer's responsibility in her representation of the pain of others: "No, I am not worthy to carry you in my voice." If Borda turns to Janis Joplin, Meabe confers with another icon of North-American counter-culture: Patti Smith and her surrealist dream of Rimbaud. Meabe's broad range of poetic forms, tones and themes is most aptly rendered in English thanks to Catherine Phil MacCarthy's malleable craft.

Castillo Suárez (1976) has been included in a Galician anthology of Basque poetry that acknowledges the importance of the *Galeuzca* pact signed in Mexico in 1944 (Kortazar 2000). This pact consisted in the mutual recognition and collaboration of the nations of *Galicia*, *Euskadi* and *Catalunya*. However, neither her poems in that anthology nor the ones she selected for *Forked Tongues* are explicitly concerned with the national cause. Suárez writes about claustrophobic urban spaces under close surveillance where our life is measured by that of our neighbours. Her characters' psychic wounds manifest themselves in tortured bodies, and the temporary relief sought in conversation, song or sex only accentuates self-deception and frustration. The relationship with the other is always mediated and displaced whether out of fear or a feeling of inadequacy. Susan Connolly captures the disturbing thrust of this poetry and renders its surprising imagery and ominous atmosphere to great effect.

Leire Bilbao (1978) has selected her poems for this anthology from *Scanner* (2011), her latest collection. She has opted for a variety of themes which show her deft handling of different tones, registers, tropes and rhythms. To this versatility Paddy Bushe responds with unsurpassed adroitness and perceptivity. Like Suárez, Bilbao delves into the alienation experienced by the individual in urban settings. She comments on the sprawl of cities and their encroachment on the natural world thus revealing her ecocritical sensitivity. Bilbao's domestic interiors recall the paintings of Edward Hopper in the mood of resignation, *ennui* and loneliness they convey and in the subtle interaction of the characters with the objects that surround them. However, there is also room for tender love and happiness in this verse, even if it is framed by social comment and an ironic slant.

Catalan Poetry

The fact that Catalonia has been an important industrial and commercial centre since the second half of the nineteenth century, alongside the concomitant nationalist aspirations of its prosperous bourgeoisie and their endorsement of the vernacular language, have no doubt contributed to the deployment of a dynamic and strong literary system of publishers, writers, critics and readers. However, Catalan women writers have not been granted the visibility one might expect in what would, otherwise, seem like a *normalized* cultural context. A collection such as Corredor-Matheos', for instance, which claims to be the *essential* anthology of contemporary Catalan poetry, does not feature a single woman among the twenty-nine writers born in the twentieth century. This suppression of women's writing has made positive action necessary in the form of women-centred anthologies such as Carme Riera's and Encarna Sant-Celoni's.

A very productive direction in the poetry of the nineteen eighties and nineties in Catalonia examined seemingly autobiographical experience together with its moral and emotional implications. This main drift persists in the early twenty-first century, although it is being enriched with alternative proposals, some of which are illustrated by the poems in *Forked Tongues*: "a more profound exploration of the narrative possibilities of the poem, which is now conceived with a longer length than the conventional epiphanic poem; an increase in the number of learned allusions; a shift of attention to a neater definition of the relationship between literature, reality and the statute of art; finally, a gradual weeding of the anecdotal elements in the poem in the benefit of a meditative style which may prove more apt for poetry of a metaphysical tenor" (Ballart and Julià).

Although Catalan-language poetry is not limited to that produced in Catalonia and has also had important writers in the Valencian Community and Balearic Islands, the already broad scope of this anthology with writers from three Iberian autonomous communities has swayed me to choose four poets from Catalonia whose first published collections have come out in the last twenty years. Apart from being a writer of poetry and essays, **Vinyet Panyella** (1954) has co-organized art exhibitions and has written on painters such as Picasso, Cézanne, Dalí, Rusiñol and El Greco. For *Forked Tongues* she has selected two poems from her 2007 collection *Taller Cézanne* [Cézanne Studio] which evince her interest in the visual arts and their possible intersections with literature: Panyella *reads* a painting and through her verse we conjure shapes, colours, lines and textures; she considers her feminine gaze in relation to that of the male masters of painting in their rendering of the female body; she inquires about the process of identification between the subject and object of representation; she instils emotions in the *silent* art of a still life. Panyella's poems from her other collections are songs of experience which delve into pain and endurance, the flux of life and identity, and the blurred line between author and text. Michael O'Loughlin's versions have none of the superfluous words or periphrases that we sometimes find in translations. While accurate and attentive to Panyella's writing, his powerful re-creation of her poems reads like an original text.

Susanna Rafart (1962) is a widely acclaimed poet and fiction writer. Her lyric style has been described as "elegant and delicate words, very well chosen and cut with precision for their place within the verse like the tesserae of a mosaic. […] free of dissonance and fanfare, vulgarity and outbursts, everything is said with the subtlety and tenderness of a cat caressing a hand" (Forcano). For *Forked Tongues*, Rafart has selected poems that dialogue with various literary traditions and, in particular, with female writers such as Emily Dickinson and Sor Juana Inés de la Cruz, with whom she shares a meditative style and a metaphysical yearning about the soul's quest. Paula Meehan excels in her rendering of Rafart's exquisite imagery and the Irish poet's accomplishment in the rhythm and rhyme patterns of poems such as "Senyor, no m'abandonis a l'amor" [Lord, do not abandon me to love] constitutes a true homage to the craft of translation.

Gemma Gorga (1968) combines the metapoetic creation that confers with literary traditions and writers from a distant time and space, as in "Llegint Matsuo Bashô" [Reading Matsuo Bashō], with poems about the proximity and complicity of bodies and the physical and emotional sensations they arouse. Keith Payne is especially effective in his attention to the pace of Gorga's phrasing and the sensorial impressions of her verse. Gemma Gorga feels at home in the liminal space between language and the real world where they nourish and inspire each other. She construes a desiring female subject who is aware of her agency in shaping her life and her relations. Susanna Rafart has said of her 2005 collection *Instruments òptics* [Optical Instruments]: "[this] is a book of poems of rewarding convalescence. Convalescence produces guiltless inaction and envisages wonder, reflection and detachment from existence. Gemma Gorga opens for us a chamber in which stillness, as a category, conjures a different realm."

Although **Mireia Calafell** (1980) is the youngest poet in this collection, her work has had a significant reception in the Catalan literary world and has already been anthologized (García, Alemany, among others). Both in her academic writing and her poetry, she has been concerned with the way the body is construed through discourse and with the inscription of identity, gender, sexuality and class, among other categories, in the body. She acknowledges the influence of former Catalan women poets such as Maria-Mercè Marçal, Montserrat Abelló, Felícia Fuster and Teresa Pascual, who have cleared the way for her as a writer. The poems she has selected for *Forked Tongues* interrogate still prevalent notions of romantic love from an ironic stance that suggests revealing comparisons with the Basque poet Leire Bilbao. Theo Dorgan handles sound patterns with a seasoned skill and masterfully conveys emotional yearning, wry humour, the sensuality of the body, and the pain of knowledge.

Some stylistic features and thematic concerns may seem recurrent in this selection of thirteen poets: free verse and speech rhythm, the prose poem, the irregularity of stanzas, the splitting of the poetic voice, the urban setting, the meditative approach, the renewal of imagery, the inter-arts analogy, the ironic stance with regard to ideals —whether public or private— and the exploration of alternative discourses about the female body, to mention a few. There are also some fascinating examples of familiar patterns of rhymes, rhythms and stanzas which evince an ongoing dialogue with literary tradition, with its tropes and subject matter. This anthology does not intend to provide a simplifying and homogenizing survey of women writers' poetry since the nineteen nineties that echoes the editor's personal taste. *Forked Tongues* celebrates the spaces of convergence —among the vernacular literatures on the one hand and between them and their English counterparts on the other— but also the divergent paths that each poet chooses to follow in her individual poetic quest.

Manuela Palacios
University of Santiago de Compostela

Works Cited

Aleixandre, Marilar. 1999. "nun coitelo de sal." *Catálogo de venenos*. Ferrol: Sociedade de Cultura Valle-Inclán. 42.

Alemany, Edgar et al. 2008. *Pedra foguera: antologia de poesia jove dels Països Catalans*. Palma de Mallorca: Documenta Balear.

Alonso, Fran. 2007. "Lupe Gómez, a provocación libertaria." *El País*. 16th March. http://elpais.com/diario/2007/03/16/galicia/1174043918_850215.html

Ballart, Pere and Jordi Julià, eds. 2005. "Prólogo." *Lírica de fin de siglo. Poesía catalana y española. 1980-2000*. Granada: Diputación de Granada. 9-15.

Boland, Eavan. 1998. "The Mother Tongue." *The Lost Land*. Manchester: Carcanet. 30-31.

Cambeiro López, Emilio Xosé. 2010. "*Livro das devoracións*, na procura do ollar pausado do mundo." *Boletín Galego de Literatura* 43: 7-27.

Casas, Arturo, ed. 2003. *Antoloxía consultada da poesía galega. 1976-2000*. Lugo: TrisTram.

——— 2011. "Producing World and Remnant: Dialogue with Chus Pato." *Performing Poetry. Body, Place and Rhythm in the Poetry Performance*. Eds. Cornelia Gräbner and Arturo Casas. Amsterdam: Rodopi. 133-150.

Corredor-Matheos, José, ed. 1983, 2001. *Antología esencial de la poesía catalana contemporánea*. Madrid: Espasa Calpe.

Ediciones La Palma. 2001. *Once (poetas) para trescientos (lectores). (Mujeres poetas en el País Vasco)*. Madrid: Ediciones La Palma.

Fernández Iglesias, Arantza. 2001. "Prólogo." *Once (poetas) para trescientos (lectores). (Mujeres poetas en el País Vasco)*. Madrid: Ediciones La Palma. 9-19.

Forcano, Manuel. 2004. "Carta a Susanna Rafart des de París." Prologue to Susanna Rafart's *Retrat en blanc*. Palma de Mallorca: Moll.

García, Concha. 2011, ed. and trans. *Noreste. Doce poetas catalanes contemporáneos*. Buenos Aires: Editorial Espacio Hudson.

Gómez, Lupe. 2005. *Azul e estranxeira*. Sada: Edicións do Castro.

González Fernández, Helena. 2005. *Elas e o paraugas totalizador. Escritoras, xénero e nación*. Vigo: Xerais.

Kortazar, Jon. 1999. *La pluma y la tierra. Poesía vasca contemporánea (1978-1995)*. Sta. Cruz de Tenerife: Las Tres Sorores, PRAMES.

———, coord. 2000. *A ponte das palabras. Poesía vasca 1990-2000 / Hitzezko zubia. Euskal poesia 1990-2000*. Compostela: Argitaletxea, Letras de Cal, A.C. Amaía.

Letras de Cal Editorial Board. 1999. "Letras limiares." *dEfecto 2000. Antoloxía de poetas dos 90*. Compostela: Letras de Cal, A.C. Amaía. 7-8.

Marramao, Giacomo. 2011. "Eguaglianza e differenza. Per una crita della democrazia identitaria." Lecture at the Consello de Cultura Galega, Santiago de Compostela. 18th November.

McGuckian, Medbh and Nuala Ní Dhomhnaill. 1995. "Comhrá, with a Foreword and Afterword by Laura O'Connor." *The Southern Review*. 31.3: 581-614.

Nogueira, María Xesús. 2003. "A poesía galega actual. Algunhas notas, necesariamente provisorias, para un estado da cuestión." *Madrygal* 6: 85-97.

O'Donnell, Mary and Manuela Palacios, eds. 2010. *To the Winds Our Sails. Irish Writers Translate Galician Poetry*. Cliffs of Moher: Salmon Poetry.

Olaziregi, Mari Jose, ed. 2007. *Six Basque Poets*. Trans. Amaia Gabantxo. Todmorden: Arc Publications.

Pato, Chus. 2000. *m-Talá*. Vigo: Xerais. (Translated into English by Erín Moure. Exeter and Ottawa: Shearsman and BuschekBooks, 2009).

Paz, Octavio. 1971. *Traducción: literatura y literalidad*. Barcelona: Tusquets.

Poetry Wales. 2008. "In Conversation: María do Cebreiro and Menna Elfyn." *Poetry Wales* 44.2: 10-14.

Rábade Villar, María do Cebreiro. 2009. "Políticas e poéticas de segunda man: A espectralidade no proceso da tradución." *Galicia 21* A: 56-67.

Rafart, Susanna. 2006. "Les veus que interroguen la veu: *Instruments òptics*, Gemma Gorga." *Lectora. Revista de dones i textualitat* 12: 180-181.

Raña, Román. 2010. "Atormentados lirismos. Con beleza innumerábel." Review of Chus Pato's *Fascinio* in *Faro de Vigo*. 14th October. http://www.aelg.org/Centrodoc/GetParatextById.do;jsessionid=F4583D5D4010D7630EFC3267C0E42BBF?id=paratext4901

Riera, Carme, ed. 2003. *Antologia de poesia catalana femenina*. Barcelona: Mediterrània.

Rodriguez Bornaetxea, Fito. 2004. "Análisis comparativo de la situación actual en la resolución política de los conflictos vasco e irlandés." Danny Morrison, *El IRA y la paz en Irlanda*. Fito Rodriguez Bornaetxea, *Los conflictos irlandés y vasco*. Hondarribia: Argitaletxe HIRU. 93-138.

Rodríguez García, José María. 2011. "Yolanda Castaño: Fashionista and Floating Poet." *Discourse* 33.1: 101-127.

Sant-Celoni i Verger, Encarna. 2008. *Erotiques i despentinades: un recorregut de cent anys per la poesia catalana amb veu de dona*. Tarragona: Arola Editors.

Stratford, Madeleine. 2011. "From 'Alejandra' to 'Susanna': Susan Bassnett's 'Life Exchange' with Alejandra Pizarnik." *Translating Women*. Ed. Luise von Flotow. Ottawa: University of Ottawa Press. 71-96.

Galician Poets

PILAR PALLARÉS

translated by

MAURICE HARMON

Matéria porosa na mañá...

(Nos Alyscamps. Arles)

Matéria porosa na mañá,
embebida de luz,
fructificada na cor da terracota.
Sen filiación,
sen nome.
Desprovista de signos e de história
ser só a que contempla,
a oferecida a toda posesión
e rapto.

...

Na hora inteira, a auséncia.
Na plenitude azul e ocre destas áleas
unha oquidade de alma,
un desexo de ser confusamente
mineral e epiderme,
de vaziar-me de min como un sarcófago,
"dulcissima et innocentissima",
vella e pequena morta, Chrisogone.

...

Vaziar-me de ser para o ser todo
ao azar de cada instante.
Devastar o pasado.
Arrancar e polir até tocar o centro
da dureza, a osamenta esencial,
o núcleo de meu nada.
Ser oco e superficie.
Deixar que as estacións de sílex e antracita
apaguen o calor da miña boca,
que toda ave me esqueza.

...

Sieved substance of morning…

(At the Alyscamps, Arles)

Sieved substance of morning,
filled with light,
made fruitful in the colour of terracotta.
Of unknown lineage,
nameless.
Deprived of history and signs
it is you alone that ponders,
given up to possession
and pillage.

...

At the heart of now, absence.
In the blue and ochre fullness of these paths
a hollowness of soul,
a longing to be both
content and shell,
to empty being like a tomb,
"dulcissima et innocentissima,"
old and little dead one, Chrisogone.

...

Drain myself of being for the entire span
at the whim of each instant.
Consume the past.
Tear up and wear down to reach the core
of hardness, the necessary bones,
the nub of my nothingness.
Be centre and surface.
Let the phases of flint and anthracite
reduce the heat of my mouth,
let each bird forget me.

...

Lugar de privación.
Nen sequer a poeira dos teus osos,
a moeda que che paga esta morada,
o artello dun crustáceo que viaxou
entre os pregues da túnica
polo curso das águas.
Da tua idade só resta este siléncio,
esta pedra gastada que non soubo gardar-te.

...

Ao final do vazio está o teu nome.
Ao final do meu nada ven a noite
coas suas vagas ferozes.
Algo, que non se detén, pasa cantando,
deixa unha nota aguda na memória do sangue.

Libro das devoracións (1996)

Place of loss.
Not even the dust-shower of your bones,
the coin that pays for this your dwelling place,
the joint of the crab that lodged
in the fold of cloth
along the course of waters.
Only this stillness prevails,
this porous rock that failed to hold you.

...

At the end of the vacuum your name.
At the end of my nothingness night
with its furious waves.
Without a pause, something goes by, singing,
leaving a high-pitched note in what the blood recalls.

Book of Voraciousness (1996)

asi é e asi sexa…

asi é e asi sexa
mentres me precipito por esta tarde imensa
e un relóxio de sol mente-me as cinco e cuarto

o peso do que perdo?
o tacto ausente da pedra?
simulacións da luz
velando o corpo inerme das crisálidas

esta hora non pasa:
despraza-se cara un borde máis difuso
ampea fatigada   morde a raiz da onda
demora-se no ventre das baleas
arrasta xabre e bránquias
regresa eternamente con cabeleiras violáceas de afogadas
co meu rosto lourido de vintetantos anos

o peso do que perdo?
a lei gravitatória do que gaño
nas águas adensadas desta hora
no entullo do que fun e que me alaga
e me desaba en ser entre os meus mortos

arxilas da memória
todo e nada
espellismos de sal que a tarde inventa

Libro das devoracións (1996)

that is how it is and so be it...

that is how it is and so be it
while I heave myself through this immense afternoon
and a sundial deceives me five fifteen

how can I measure what I lose?
the missing feel of stone?
simulations of light
guarding the lifeless body of the chrysalis

this hour does not pass:
shifts towards a less reliable edge
pants exhausted   bites the heart of the wave
dawdles in the guts of whales
drags weed and gills
returns endlessly with the violet spirits of drowned women
with my wan face of twenty-odd years

how can I measure what I lose?
the irresistible pull of what I gain
in the dense waters of this hour
in the silt of what I have been, what floods through me
and drenches my being with my dead

clay of memory
all and nothing
salt shapes the afternoon begets

Book of Voraciousness (1996)

O desexo era un lóstrego…

O desexo era un lóstrego
que nos alzaba unánimes cara un ceu de sangue
partido polo raio.

Os astros tiñan pel
e respiraban,
pugnaban por ser un cos pés no abismo.

Pairámos sobre a dor e a cor dos mapas.
Un continente en branco,
unha sabana inmensa a agardar por un nome.

Balbuciámos palabras inauditas.
Éramos deuses novos, e morrían
sen chegaren á terra.

Caímos ao mencer
en lados diferentes da fronteira da vida.

Leopardo son (2011)

Desire, a lightning strike…

Desire, a lightning strike
lifted us as one towards a blood-red sky
torn by a bolt.

Stars which had flesh
and breath
sought a foothold in the abyss.

We were stuck in the pain and stain of charts.
A spotless space,
a vast savannah waiting to be inscribed.

We mumbled words no one heard.
We were young bloods, and they faded
without finding earth.

We came down at dawn
on opposite sides of life's frontier.

Leopard Being (2011)

CHUS PATO

translated by

LORNA SHAUGHNESSY

Un paxaro, unha dama, un león, unha aguia, un anxo, un corazón, un horizonte

O paxaro baila todos os días na rompente
é un paxaro pero nada nel é diferente da escuma

algún día un corazón deixará de ser escuma

un corazón
cre que é verao
e é certo
todos os días son verao
todos os días pode mergullarse no mar Negro

a liña que debuxa
o paxaro
afástase e regresa
é un ritmo
(por iso dicimos que a casa do paxaro é un ritmo)
constrúe dous hemisferios simétricos
o ecuador é a rompente
e expándese en sentido horizontal
é un deseño lanceolado

este cerebro é a casa do corazón

é a folla dunha árbore
dun álamo

pero a folla levita sobre a galla

ninguén pedirá o bautismo
ninguén lembrará o mesías

a casa do paxaro son os álamos

O ritmo do ollo (unpublished)

A bird, a lady, a lion, an eagle, an angel, a heart, a horizon

The bird dances every day where the waves break
it is a bird but in no way different from the foam

some day a heart will cease to be foam

a heart
believes it is summer
and it's true
every day is a summer
every day it can plunge into the Black sea

the line traced by
the bird
moves away and comes back again
is a rhythm
(that's why we say the bird's house is a rhythm)
it builds two symmetrical hemispheres
the equator is the shore where the waves break
and it spreads in a horizontal motion
to make a lanceolate shape

this brain houses the heart

it is the leaf of a tree
of a poplar

but the leaf hovers over the forking branch

no-one will ask for baptism
no-one will remember the messiah

the poplars are the house of the bird

The Rhythm of the Eye (unpublished)

Eleusis

Isto
eu
aquí
agora
ti
hoxe
mañá
entón
o mesmo día
sempre

nada hai na voz nada

unha lingua de fogo que a todos e a cada unha pertence

pero quen di o idioma é a voz
non está
e volve

O ritmo do ollo (unpublished)

Eleusis

This
I
here
now
you
today
tomorrow
then
the same day
always

there is nothing in the voice nothing

a tongue of fire that belongs to each and every one

but whoever pronounces the language is the voice
that is absent
and returns

The Rhythm of the Eye (unpublished)

Claridade de xuízo

Entendo que a vida é o que vivimos: esta a túa a miña a nosa vida
entendo que un poema é pobreza si se mide coa vida
entendo que é pausa
que por un instante separa a vida de si
que pesa e fai balance
esguiza os sentidos
impropio
un vértice corpóreo
Entendo que é acceso ao intelecto
Así o entendo
que o poema indica a desconexión entre melodía e sentido
Entendo que un poema só se escribe con versos finais
Desfonda o idioma
desfonda a vida

O ritmo do ollo (unpublished)

Clear-Sighted

I understand that life is what we live: this your my our life
I understand the poverty of a poem when measured against life
I understand it is a pause
that for an instant parts life from itself
weighs it up
scratches at the senses
inappropriate
a corporeal apex
I understand it is the way to the intellect
This much I understand
that a poem points to the disjuncture between melody and meaning
that a poem is written only with last lines
collapses language
collapses life

The Rhythm of the Eye (unpublished)

Corazón

É tan lixeiro o espello que a súa decisión é voar
quere pensar un ceo:
alto altísimo celeste grande grandísimo
en contacto
unha grandeza
(é agora cando se nos revela un ínfimo cristal)
Nada disto pode escribirse:
o xesto que traza a liberdade e a liberdade dos límites
O espello bate
prega sobre si a musculatura
torce en hélice e finalmente volvese encartar
A grandeza
que non garda relación coa medida
pénsase no corazón
"tes que termar das augas
a súa decisión é voar"
Nada se semella ao mundo
que é separado e desigual e outro
mundo único que é
Nunca remata nunca o inferno
e nunca é verdade
Como a sombra do ceo nas augas
e do bosque no ceo das augas
rítmico
como un día de néboa
É enxoito permanecer aquí
(un deserto abrasa calquera crenza e tamén a fortaleza abrasa)
é ceibe agudo estreito

O ritmo do ollo (unpublished)

Heart

The mirror is so light it aims to fly
it means to conjure up a sky:
high highest celestial vast vastness
touching
a greatness
(only now it reveals itself as humble glass)
None of this can be written down:
the gesture that traces freedom and the freedom of limits
The mirror flaps
folds muscle in on itself
turns in circular motion and finally folds again
The greatness
that bears no relation to measurement
is thought up in the heart
"you have to hold on tight to the waters
they aim to fly away"
Nothing is like the world
that is separate and unequal and other
unique world that is
Hell never ends ever
and it is never true
Like the sky's shadow in the waters
and the woods in the sky in the waters
rhythmic
as a foggy day
Just here it is dry
(a desert burns belief and fortitude also burns)
is free sharp narrow

The Rhythm of the Eye (unpublished)

LUPE GÓMEZ ARTO

translated by

ANNE LE MARQUAND HARTIGAN

TENDA DE COSMÉTICOS

No meu pobo

só había un costume,

camiñar co pelo solto

e os peitos caídos.

Pornografía (1995)

MAKING UP

In my village

there was only one custom,

walking out with one's hair flowing

and breasts falling free.

Pornography (1955)

ENFOQUE TEÓRICO

A muller é

un cristal

atravesado por

unha patria.

Pornografía (1995)

A CLINICAL STARE

The woman is

a crystal

pierced through

by a fatherland.

Pornography (1995)

ROAD MOVIE

A escrita dun texto é como unha *road movie*. Saes dun lugar e chegas a mundos distintos, que se van enredando uns cos outros como cereixas. O zume de laranxa é tan nutritivo como escribir un texto literario. Vou coa miña amiga Xohana Torres nun coche enorme. Imos tan contentas como os reloxos cando están parados. Non nos importa o sur nin o norte. Trátase dunha viaxe ao infinito. Visitamos unha cidade que é unha obra de teatro. Paramos para coller gasolina nunha montaña abandonada. Escribimos un poema coas mans molladas. Debuxamos unha nube cos nosos ollos cegos. "Non quero coñecerte. Prefiro que falemos nas cartas, sen chegar a vernos, porque resulta máis misterioso" díxome unha vez a miña amiga Xohana. Na película *Paris-Texas* de Wim Wenders todo sucede de forma rápida e desordenada como na creación literaria. Tiven un bo mestre na Universidade: Arturo Casas. Con el aprendín que as palabras son viaxes que facemos co corpo, coa imaxinación e coa memoria. Os cemiterios son *road movies*. "Bienaventurados los que descansan en el Señor, porque ellos serán afortunados." As cereixas son froitas de verán. Alimentan moitísimo, tanto como a prosa poética e a historia da filosofía. Só vin a Xohana unha vez na miña vida. Estivemos sentadas nos sofás do Casino, e decidimos coller os noso coche enorme para visitar Bilbao, Barcelona e París. Manexamos moi ben o volante, falamos todos os idiomas posíbeis e somos mulleres atravesadas por unha patria. Antonio Gamoneda escribiume unha carta: "Mis estanterías tienen tres o más metros de literatura en gallego, lengua que amo." Non hai regreso posíbel cando decides navegar polo mar nunha *road movie*. Ao final da viaxe, as cereixas viven no exilio.

Diálogos imposíbeis (2010)

ROAD MOVIE

Writing is like a *road movie*. You leave one place and go to different worlds, which wind and twine around each other like cherries. Orange juice is as good for you as writing a literary piece. I go with my friend Xohanna Torres in an enormous car. We go along happy and contented as watches when they have stopped. Neither south nor north matters to us. This is our journey into infinity. We find a city that is a theatre piece. We stop for petrol in an abandoned mountain. We write a poem with wet hands. With blind eyes we draw a cloud. "I don't want to know you. I prefer us to talk in letters, without actually seeing each other, because it's more mysterious" my friend Xohana said to me once. In the film *Paris-Texas* by Wim Wenders everything happens rapidly and in a disordered way like in creative writing. I had a good teacher at the University: Arturo Casas. With him I learned that words are journeys we make in our body, in our imaginations and in our memory. Cemeteries are *road movies*. "Fortunate are those who rest in the Lord, for they will be blessed." Cherries are summer fruits. They are enormously nourishing, just like poetic prose and the history of philosophy. I only saw Xohana once in my life. We were sitting on the sofas in the Casino, and we decided to take our huge car to visit Bilbao, Barcelona and Paris. We drove, lightly holding the steering wheel, we spoke in all possible languages and we are women crossed over by a fatherland. Antonio Gamoneda wrote me a letter, "My shelves have three or more metres of literature in Galician, a language I love." There is no way possible to return when you decide to navigate by sea in a *road movie*. At the end of the journey, the cherries are exiled.

Impossible Dialogues (2010)

Doce canción de chuvia acompaña un aire de violetas
(Xohana)

POZO

Gustaríame que a fantasía enchese
os nosos pulmóns e as nosas vidas.
"La tierra es un pozo que come violetas."
Nas piscinas de plástico a auga sabe
como se fose un conto de risa.
"No llores cuando te tiren piedras.
No te encojas en ti misma cuando
los trenes vengan muy despacio."

Fantasía e sangue de papoulas.
Entrar no pozo e levar no bolso
unha variña máxica para transformar
as traxedias. Romper a caixa de costura.
As máscaras son tan necesarias como
a poesía de Xohana Torres. Tes as mans
lavadas? Sabes tocar a pandeireta?

O pozo é tan profundo como un poema.
A música sae entre as pedras… Queres medrar
para ser alta, ou prefires seguir sendo pequena?
Teño un lapis de ollos para pintar as paredes.
Tocan as campás e enchen o aire de perfume.

Manteño correspondencia coa miña sobriña
de tres anos. Ela non sabe escribir nin ler.
Escribirlle cartas faime inmensamente feliz.
Teño catro irmáns e catro sobriños. Somos
unha familia numerosa. A fantasía vive
nos tranvías e na doce canción de chuvia.
Durmir moito é a mellor medicina para

Sweet song of rain accompanies an air of violets
                                            (Xohana)

WELL

I'd like dream to fill
our lungs and our lives,
"The earth is a well that swallows violets."
In plastic swimming pools the water tastes
as if it were a comic story.
"Don't cry when they throw stones into you.
Don't shrink into yourself when
the trains are very late."

Dreams and blood of poppies.
Jump into the well and carry in your bag
a magic wand to transform
tragedies. Smash the sewing box.
Masks are as necessary
as the poetry of Xohana Torres. Have you washed
your hands? Can you play the tambourine?

The well is as deep as a poem.
The music seeps out from between the stones… Do you want
to grow up to be tall, or do you prefer to carry on being little?
I have an eye liner to paint the walls.
Bells are ringing and filling
the air with perfume.

I hold a correspondence with my niece
who's three years old. She can't read or write.
Writing letters to her makes me immensely happy.
I have four siblings and four nieces and nephews. We are
a large family. Dreams live
in the trams and in the sweet song of the rain.
Sleeping a lot is the best medicine to

estar de bo humor... Gustaríame ser
a noiva dun elefante AFRICANO.

No escenario unha figura de Sargadelos fai o pinchacarneiro.

Diálogos imposíbeis (2010)

be in a good mood... I'd just love to be
the bride of an AFRICAN elephant.

On the stage a Sargadelos figure does a somersault

Impossible Dialogues (2010)

YOLANDA CASTAÑO

translated by

MÁIGHRÉAD MEDBH

Pero eu, filla das miñas fillas...

Pero eu, filla das miñas fillas, hei desmantelar a golpe de deslumbramentos esta aciaga militancia dunha yolanda emigrante de min. Eu, a soberana estéril, a por desgraza egoísta. Debo taxar a dose exacta de memoria e esquezo. Así a miña visión da verea é un rostro dende atrás. Todas as escuras raizames que se nacen en min. Non hai dirección que non me conteña, raza que non en min se comece e filas de díxitos estendendo para min os seus dedos ferais. O que interesa son os meus pasos. Coma un bosque de símbolos do que a miña ignorancia é significativa. Moito deixarse a pel pero eu non quixen aprender a chegar. Xardín exiguo, vento pechado de mans, infinita cuadrícula. Renuncio ó lugar do alento. Quero aprender a saír.

Hai tempo que un animal vive nutríndose do esquezo. Pero eu son a ventrílocua, eu, a tirana louca, a analfabeta. Co magnífico libro das venturas agochado na vulva. A que non comprendeu nada pero sentiuno todo. Son a ventrílocua, a que corre cantando polos corredores de chumbo, con voz de pizarra. E abortar foi unha obriga, unha necesidade fonda, un desafío. Para cando o pálido manto da miña memoria se vai cubrindo desta pel que eu serei. Que todas as noites con devoción escribo arrebatadoras cartas de amor e nas madrugadas panexíricos a esta yolanda mesquiña, que <u>sabe</u> venderse e   coñece o final.

Son eu na cripta e o meu nome dentro debuxado de tiza. Habitacións concéntricas. Que a miña intelixencia non compre o meu sentido. O tacto, o privilexio, as ganas de tirarse. Nin a miña cabeza será escrava do meu orgullo. Yolanda a soldada, a comerciante. Porque eu son a que nin agarda. Son o auriga do ardente carro. A egoísta porque está soa. Que tanta calamidade me satisfai, porque a miña beleza fundará dinastías. E entón será ir cunha minuciosidade de devota recolleitando eses minúsculos e ditosos pedaciños de espello roto que eu son. Yolanda farame un fogar paupérrimo entre os seus brazos de mundo e así aprenderei a inenarrable alegría de ter casa.

E entón virá ese postremeiro advento e A VerbA farase carne. E eu direi: " Eu son a da única estirpe de Adnaloy, a que estenderá os seus dedos flamíxeros sobre o horizonte, a que baixará e despois se despoxará do seu manto e vestirá un saial, e logo reclinarase e dará de comer o seu corazón ás bestas".

Yo es otro. Autorretratos de la Nueva Poesía (2001)

But I, daughter of my daughters...

But I, daughter of my daughters, will dismantle by sheer dazzle this unfortunate conformity of a yolanda émigrée. I, the sterile sovereign, egotist by misadventure. I must weigh the exact dose of memory and oblivion. So I see the path with a view from behind. All the dark roots that are born in me. There is no direction that does not contain me, race that does not rise in me and armies of cyphers reaching for me with primitive fingers. I study my steps. Like a forest of symbols I cannot fathom. Much shedding of skin though I never wished to arrive. Meagre garden, wind trapped in the hands, infinite grid. I renounce the home of this breath. I wish I knew how to leave.

For a long time an animal has fattened on the glut of oblivion. But I am the ventriloquist, I, the lunatic tyrant, the illiterate. With the magnificent book of adventures crouched in the vulva. She who understood nothing but felt all. I am the ventriloquist, she who runs singing through the leaden corridors with a voice of slate. Abortion was a duty, a serious necessity, a defiance. So that the pale robe of my memory might cloak itself in the skin I would become. You see every night devotedly I write rapturous love letters and at daybreak panegyrics to this greedy yolanda, who <u>knows</u> how to sell herself and   knows where it will end.

It is me in the crypt and my name etched inside with chalk. Concentric rooms. That my intellect may not bribe my sense. The touch, the privilege, the need to hurl oneself. Nor will my head pander to my pride. Yolanda the soldier, the trader. Because neither am I she who waits. I am the driver of the flaming chariot. An egotist because she is solo. Whose pain is pleasure because this beauty will found dynasties. And then with the meticulous attention of an ascetic I will reclaim those miniscule and charmed fragments of broken mirror that I am. Yolanda will build me a hovel in the world between her arms and I will learn there the untold happiness of being home.

Behold the last coming when the feminine will be made Word. I will proclaim: "I am the sole scion of Adnaloy, she who will stretch her flaming fingers over the horizon, who will descend, discard her gown, clothe herself in sackcloth, and thereafter lie down, rendering her heart to the appetite of beasts."

I Is Other. Self-Portraits of New Poetry (2001)

CORRUPCIÓN

Camiñar con escafandro
cun quilo de peso en cada bota
o reino das veladas alianzas
comigo ou contra min
e sáeme ao paso
este súpeto naufraxio esta
fame perplexa
que perde mapas e maneiras e, coma
besta aterrada no medio dun incendio,

agárrase ao que pode.

Profundidade de campo (2007)

CORRUPTION

Pilgrim in a diving suit
each boot a kilo's weight
the kingdom of veiled alliances
now for me now against me
then across my path
this sudden sinking this
perplexed hunger
that jettisons maps and modes and, like
a terrified beast trapped in a blaze,

clings to what power it can.

Depth of Field (2007)

HISTORIA DA TRANSFORMACIÓN

Foi primeiro un trastorno
unha lesiva abstinencia de nena eramos pobres e non tiña nin aquilo
raquítica de min depauperada antes de eu amargor carente unha
parábola de complexos unha síndrome unha pantasma
(Aciago a partes iguais botalo en falla ou lamentalo)
Arrecife de sombra que rompe os meus colares.
Foi primeiro unha branquia evasiva que
non me quixo facer feliz tocándome co seu sopro
son a cara máis común do patio do colexio
a faciana eslamiada que nada en nada sementa
telo ou non o tes renuncia afaite traga iso
corvos toldando nubes unha condena de frío eterno
unha paciente galerna unha privada privación
(nena de colexio de monxas que fun saen todas
anoréxicas ou lesbianas a
letra entra con sangue nos cóbados nas cabezas nas
conciencias ou nas conas).
Pechei os ollos e desexei con todas as miñas forzas
lograr dunha vez por todas converterme na que era.

Pero a beleza corrompe. A beleza corrompe.
Arrecife de sombra que gasta os meus colares.
Vence a madrugada e a gorxa contén un presaxio.
Pobre parviña!, obsesionácheste con cubrir con aspas en vez de
co seu contido.
Foi un lento e vertixinoso agromar de flores en inverno
Os ríos saltaban cara atrás e resolvíanse en fervenzas rosas
borboletas e caracois nacéronme nos cabelos
O sorriso dos meus peitos deu combustible aos aeroplanos
A beleza corrompe
A beleza corrompe
A tersura do meu ventre escoltaba á primavera
desbordaron as buguinas nas miñas mans tan miúdas
o meu afago máis alto beliscou o meu ventrículo
e xa non souben qué facer con tanta luz en tanta sombra.

HISTORY OF THE TRANSFORMATION

In the beginning it was a disorder
a dangerous deficiency as a girl we were poor and I didn't even own that
a rickety version of me deprived before I bitterness a lack
parable of complexes a syndrome a phantasm
(Tragic either way whether lacked or lamented)
Coral reefs of shadows that smash my pearls.
In the beginning it was an elusive gill that
made me unhappy strumming me with its breath
I am the plainest girl in the schoolyard
the graceless countenance that neither sows nor reaps
you either have it or you don't give up live with it swallow that
a storm-sky of crows a sentence of eternal cold
a chastened north-west wind a private prison
(like any convent girl they all end up
anorexic or lesbian
spare the rod spoil the child drummed into skulls into
consciences into cunts).
I closed my eyes and fervently wished
to convert forever into she who I was.

But beauty corrupts. Beauty corrupts.
Coral reefs of shadows that plunder my pearls.
Dawn comes conquering with a portent in its gaping throat.
Poor fool! you obsessed with ticking the boxes instead of
what it all meant.
It was a slow dizzy winter flowering.
The rivers leapt back and resolved to pink cascades
butterflies and winkles were born in my hair
The smile on my breasts launched aeroplanes
Beauty corrupts
Beauty corrupts
The silk of my belly ushered in the spring
conches flooded my oh so tiny hands
the high adulation gnawed at my gut
and I was frozen by light in my place of shade.

Dixéronme: "a túa propia arma será o teu propio castigo"
cuspíronme na cara as miñas propias virtudes neste
club non admiten a rapazas cos beizos pintados de vermello
un maremoto sucio unha usura de perversión que
non pode ter que ver coa miña máscara de pestanas os
ratos subiron ao meu cuarto luxaron os caixóns da roupa branca
litros de ferralla alcatrán axexo ás agachadas litros
de control litros de difamadores quilos de suspicacias levantadas
só coa tensión do arco das miñas cellas deberían maniatarte
adxudicarche unha estampa gris e borrarche os trazos con ácido
¿renunciar a ser eu para ser unha escritora?
demonizaron o esguío e lanzal do meu pescozo e o
xeito en que me nace o cabelo na parte baixa da caluga neste
club non admiten a rapazas tan ben adobiadas
Desconfiamos do estío
A beleza corrompe.
Mira ben se che compensa todo isto.

Profundidade de campo (2007)

They told me: "you will fall by your own weapon."
they spat my virtues in my face in this
club they don't admit girls with painted red lips
obscene tide perverse usury that
has nothing to do with my eyelash mascara the
rats climbed to my rooms and polluted the linen drawers
litres of scrap metal tar primed for the ambush litres
of control litres of slanderers kilos of suspicion raised
only by the draw of my arched eyebrows they should shackle you
award you the grey stamp of demerit and wipe your traces with acid
Renounce what I am to be a writer?
they demonised the gentle and svelte of my neck and the
way in which the hair springs from the nape in this
club they don't admit girls so well-endowed
The summer disconcerts us
Beauty corrupts.
Take care that it's all worth it.

Depth of Field (2007)

MARÍA DO CEBREIRO

translated by

MARY O'DONNELL

POESÍA ERÓTICA

Coa intelixencia, agora.
Non coas mans.

A loita ás veces gáñase na mente.

As mulleres escriben.

O poema ten corpo.
O amor non ten medida.

Ningúen falou de amor neste poema.

Os hemisferios (2006)

EROTIC POETRY

With your intelligence, now.
Not with the hands.

The contest is sometimes won in the mind.

Women record.

The poem has body.
Love has no metre.

Nobody mentioned love in this poem.

The Hemispheres (2006)

Eran follas pequechas...

Eran follas pequechas,
se cadra de carballo,
non sei ben.
Apareceron xuntas
onda o río.
Non igual ca unha
ofrenda, pero tenras.
Fixéronme lembrar
o seu consello: "non
esquezas o corpo".
Como se a intelixencia
fose o único obstáculo
que debía
vencer. (De certo,
non era o único.)
Pero como facer
que as palabras se abran
como follas?
Se o soubésemos penso
que non escribiríamos.
Porque non hai
talento para
a rabia, senón só rabia.
Non hai sensualidade,
senón cousas sensuais.
O que el dixo daquela
non pode transmitirse
e no espello do río
non canta o noso amor.

(unpublished)

They were little leaves…

They were little leaves,
they could have been oak,
I couldn't tell.
They appeared together
by the river.
Not quite an offering,
but fragile.
They made me recall
his advice: "don't forget
the body."
As if intelligence
were the only impediment
to conquer. (At least,
not the only one.)
But how to write
so that words
open like leaves?
If that was in our span
I think we would never write.
Because there is no gift
for rage, beyond rage itself.
There is no sensuality,
only sensual objects.
What he spoke back then
cannot be reflected,
and in the river's mirror
no song to our love.

(unpublished)

EUROPA (CUARTO REICH)

Este é o tempo
no que as mulleres pregan
para que os seus irmáns
suban á superficie,
o tempo
no que á fin coñecemos
no seu rostro a pegada do carbón
(foi indigno mirar),
o tempo no que
seguimos amando
a cor do viño, e cada noite
seguimos desexando
regresar
ao noso propio corpo
e o seu corpo
está lonxe.
Este é o tempo no que
cada un de nós
quedou ollando
para as súas propias mans,
e quixo preguntar:
para que serven?
(Para que serve a chuvia?)
Iso non o sabemos. Aínda
non foi aberta a noz
do tempo. Neste outono,
no que só choverá
de cando en vez,
pero con moita
forza, como dentro do alcol,
como no desamor
do borracho de *Embaixo
do volcán*. (E se o libro
puidese saír de ti,
como nos falaría?).
Esas cousas importan,

EUROPE (FOURTH REICH)

This is the time
when women pray
that their brothers
may ascend to the surface,
the time
when at last we see
in their faces the smears of coal
(looking lacked dignity),
the time when
we continue to love
the colour of wine, and each night
still wish to return
to our own body
while his
is so distant.
This is the era
every one of us
looked down
at her own hands,
wanting to ask:
what are they for?
(What is rain for?)
That is unknowable. Even so
the walnut of time
did not open. In this autumn,
when rain will fall
only now and again,
but with force,
like alcohol,
like the carelessness
of the drunk in *Beneath
the Volcano*. (And if the book
could emerge from you,
how would it speak to us?)
Those things count,

como quero pensar
que aínda hai algo dentro
dos últimos poemas,
que seguimos
aquí
porque a nosa conciencia
é temporal
e porque estamos vivos
e o traballo das mans medra
na nosa mente
para poder entrar no corazón
do mundo.

Poemas históricos (2010)

since I'd like to think
that something still rests
within final poems,
that we are
still here
because conscience
is temporal
and because we are alive
and the work of the hands thrives
in our minds
in order to penetrate the heart
of the world.

Historical Poems (2010)

BASQUE POETS

ITXARO BORDA

translated by

CELIA DE FRÉINE

MILIA LASTUR REVISITED
1985

Hilotzen karrasiak josirik ahoan
Nola aurkituko dun hire sokorria?
Maiteko haut Milia ez hadila joan
Hator edan dezagun ardao gorria…

Baratz aberatsetan ebatsi sagarrak
Gordeko ditinagu bide bazterretan.
Ahantz otoi Milia sarraski zaharrak
Eta suaren kantak bizihats erretan.

Belar bustietako maitasun ohantzan
Etzanen gaitun gero bi biak bihotza
Gauero zazpi itzal ikusteko dantzan.

Non dago harria? Non dago lur hotza?
Eresi hark ziona jartzeko zalantzan
Maiteko haut Milia ez hadila lotsa…

Krokodil bat daukat bihotzaren ordez (1986)

MILIA OF LASTUR REVISITED
1985

How will you find salvation with
The cries of cadavers bound to your lips?
I will love you, Milia, don't go.
Come, let's drink this blood-red wine…

And hide by the wayside the apples
Plundered from ample orchards.
Forget, please, Milia, your old wound
And the fiery chants that scorched lives.

Then, my love, the two of us will lie
Down together on a bed of moist grass
To watch the seven shades dance each night.

Where is the slab? Where the cold earth?
To give lie to what is sung in this old lament,
I will love you, Milia. Don't be afraid…

I Have a Crocodile for a Heart (1986)

BE MY WOMAN

Beha iezadan
Ahurren egitik mintzo natzain
Aukeratuagatik partitzea zaila
Dela ulertzen duen
      Bakarra haiz
      Ez nazan utzi
Be my woman.

Beha iezadan
Bularren hegitik mintzo natzain
Aspertu gabe nire ezin egon latza
Onetsi dezakeen
      Bakarra haiz
      Ez nazan utzi
Be my woman.

Beha iezadan
Sabelen begitik mintzo natzain
Irritik Janis Joplin eta Judith Butler
Bat direla dakien
      Bakarra haiz
      Ez nazan utzi
Be my woman.

Beha iezadan
Gorputz alegitik mintzo natzain
Atsegin oldetik mendea ukamen
Datorrela dioen
      Bakarra haiz
      Ez nazan utzi
Be my woman.

(unpublished)

BE MY WOMAN

Look at me
I speak to you from my outstretched palms
Only you understand
It's hard to part
    Though this is what you've chosen
    Don't leave me
Be my woman.

Look at me
I speak to you from the heft of my breast
Only you endure
My awful need
    Without tedium
    Don't leave me
Be my woman.

Look at me
I speak to you from the depth of my womb
Only you know
Janis Joplin and Judith Butler
    Have the same laugh
    Don't leave me
Be my woman.

Look at me
I speak from the body's imposture
Only you insist
This wave of pleasure
    Will lead to an age of denial
    Don't leave me
Be my woman.

(unpublished)

KARTZ

Gauaren erdian hire irriak nigan
Kartz harriaren pare
Oihar egiten din
Luzaz
Luzaz
Eta iraun dezan
Gauaren erdian hire irriak nigan
Ezpainak
Ukitzen deztenat
Behatz soilaz
Luzaz
Luzaz
Nik ere
Oihar egin dezadan
Kartz harriaren pare
Hire irriarekin bat gauaren erdian
Betiko ez baldin bada
Luzaz
Bederen.

(unpublished)

QUARTZ

Your laughter in me in the middle of the night
Resonates like
The quartz stone
For a long time
For a long time
And to sustain
Your laughter in me in the middle of the night
With fingertips
I caress
Your lips
For a long time
For a long time
So that I too
Resonate like
The quartz stone
With your laughter in the middle of the night
If not forever
At least
For a long time.

(unpublished)

MARIA MERCEREN (B)EGIA

Urtea eman dinat hire hitzak biltzen.
Ene mintzairan ere ez hintzen isiltzen.
Elerik samurrenak nintinan ibiltzen
Eskail nagiaz itsu, mirail birilbiltzen.

Hire begia zunan, lotsarikan gabe,
Zabaltzen azkorrian, argiaren jabe:
So urratua zohar, batzutan herabe,
Egin dinat munduaz amodio habe.

Gatzaren andereak ditizten girgiltzen
Baina aritzen gaitun tipulak bipiltzen
Heriotzari trufaz, oraindik nerabe.

Dugun kanta bizia, aditzen norabe,
Berma dakigun egi biluzien labe:
Urtea eman dinat hirekilan hiltzen.

(unpublished)

THE EYE OF MARIA-MERCÈ MARÇAL

I have spent the year gathering your words
Even as they found voice in my tongue.
Blinded by the indolent mote I have used
The blandest phrases to polish the mirror.

But your eye, in no way overawed, opened
At dawn in answer to the master of light:
Daunted, at times, by that clear rent vision,
I have made of the world a beam of love.

The tinkle of crystal is heard as women emerge
From the salt—we continue to peel onions,
Laughing at death, adolescent evermore.

May our song of life, framed in verbs,
Become an oven in which to bake the bare truth:
I have spent the year dying with you.

(unpublished)

OUTSIDE

Outside nago.
Has been baino has behin
bat baizik ez naiz
oraindik ere.
        Ene poesia
        a-soziala
        dela
dinotsut
outsidera
deitzen zaitudan
bitartean.
Ez dut laudatiorik nahi
basamortuan oihuz dabilan
ahots alderraia
baizik ez naizelako
oraindik ere.
        Ene poesia
        a-soziala
        dela
dinotsut.
Ez dut ezagupenik nahi
ez egun, ez bihar, ez etzi,
basamortuan kantari dabilan
sakrifikatuaren itzal
alderraia
baizik ez naizela
dagoeneko.
        Ene poesia
        a-soziala
        dela
dinotsut.
No future outside:
Ahantzi dezatela
        Ene poesia
        a-soziala

OUTSIDE

I am outside
a beginner   rather
than a has-been.
      I tell you
      my poetry
      is
      a-social
When
I invite you
to come outside.
I don't want honour
because I am   but
the voice of a nomad
howling
in the desert.
      I tell you
      my poetry
      is
      a-social.
I don't want recognition
not today or tomorrow
or the day after
because from now on I am   but
the shade of a sacrificial nomad
chanting
in the desert.
      I tell you
      my poetry
      is
      a-social.
No future outside:
may my
      a-social
      poetry

gure amen izerdiak
ahantzi diren bezala.
Amen.

(unpublished)

be forgotten
as our mothers' sweat
has been.
Amen.

(unpublished)

MIREN AGUR MEABE

translated by

CATHERINE PHIL MACCARTHY

Zisnearen kantua

Zenbat balio du gutxi jakin nahi eta
ezer eskatzen ez duen emakume batek?

Esku-ahurrak gora begira ditu,
eta zeruak adurra askatzen du, errukior.

Hileko odolari, iraganaren akronimo horri,
seme nerabearen tristura elkartu zaio.

Kantuan ari da zisnea, mezurik sentituena
hormonen ilunabarrean.

Teilapeetan, amodioak gogaitu eta elikaturiko bizitzak,
bodegoi sepia eta berdeak, bakea eta gerra lore artean.

Hain da hauskorra dena, hain erraza laburbiltzen.
Edukia eta edukiontzia, naufragio bakoitzaren markak.

Bitsa eskuetan (2010)

Swan Song

At what cost does a woman not want
to know and not ask for anything?

The palms of the hands have looked upwards,
and the sky lets flow manna, in compassion.

The period, that acronym of the past,
coincides with the sadness of the teenage son.

A swan is singing the most deeply felt melody,
the twilight of the hormones.

Under the roofs, love vexes and nurtures the lives,
still-life in green and sepia, war and peace among flowers.

Everything is so fragile, so easy, so abbreviated.
Belongings and their shell, the traits of a shipwrecked life.

Foam in Your Hands (2010)

Patti Smith Rimbaudekin ametsetan

Patti Smith liluratu egin zen Rimbaudekin. Poema bat idatzi zion, amets bat, non aipatzen zituen Charleville eta Abisinia, soroak, ur-putzuak, zauri bat begian kristal batez egina, esku handiak, masail gorriztak, logela bat, begirada ustez axolagabeak. Arthur belauniko, negarrez, belaunetatik helduz Pattiri. Patti ohean etzanda, iletik helduz Arthurri. Sugarra dira ilea eta biloa, o Jesus! Orratzak atzamarrak, o Jesus! Zeurea naiz osorik.

Horraino poemaren laburpen badaezpadakoa. Eta horren harira, neure txanda.

Andre birloka naiz. Uztaila da, zapatu bazkalostea, neure baratzean, atea ertirekirik. Zozo-bikotea palmondoaren ezkatetan, moko laranjekin eltxo bila. Etzanda nago olanazko jarlekuan. Labandaren firfira. Ura ipini behar dut tea egiteko. Eskutik labain egin dit Pattiren poema-liburuak. Rimbauden antologia elebiduna Bilbon daukat. Hara, lagun hark oparitu zidan, otso-lanak egiten zituenak, nire 45. urtebetetzean, eta horrexekin izorratu ninduen zeharo. Hain nengoen burbuila uherra bihurtua, punp egiteko irrikaz, hain nintzen jostura gaizki lotua, urratzeko desiraz. Halaxe agintzen zuen bizitzak orduan, esan dezagun, nahiz eta kontua ez den, inondik ere, batere xinplea, batere.

Marigorringoek kilimak egiten dizkidate bernetan, eta uraz pentsatzen dut, ahoa lehor. Hola, guapa, esan dit etorri denak. Ahots hori aiztoa da arrastirian, o Jesus! Gaixorik egon zara, printzesa, neuk prestatuko dut tea, masajea emango oinetan, sandaliak kentzen lagunduko, zu lasai, sirena ilegorria. Azukre epela bihurtu zait txistua. Ezin begirik ireki, indarge ni begi berdantzetan dzanga egiteko.

Hotzikara eragin dit koilaratxoak bular artean. Kikara beroan sartu ditu berak atzamarrak, intziri bat ito du. Ezpainetan ditut orain haren hatz luzeak. Zantar hori. Txupatu egiten dizkit belaunak bere lixazko mihiarekin. Mahaspasa eta ronezko izozkiak dituzu belaunak, Meibi, maybe, agian, Meabe, akaso. Goazen barrura, ez egin dar-dar. Ahotsarekin irentsi nau, galdua ni marraxoaren eztarrian.

Parasma-metxak hagetan, planeta burdinkarak erlojuetan, txori-hezurrak altzarietan.

Patti Smith Dreams of Rimbaud

Patti Smith was fascinated by Rimbaud. She wrote him a poem, a dream, where she speaks of Charleville and Abyssinia, fields, well-springs, a wound in the eye inflicted with a splinter of glass, large hands, red cheeks, a bedroom, apparently indifferent eyes. Arthur on his knees, crying, embracing Patti's knees. Patti lying in bed, grasps Arthur's hair. The flames are hair and fuzz, Oh Jesus! The fingers, needles. Oh, Jesus! I am yours entirely.

So far the dubious summary of the poem, and the next thread, my turn.

I am a woman, possessed. July, a Saturday, early afternoon in my garden, the door ajar. A pair of blackbirds probe in the blades of the palm, with orange beaks, looking for mosquitoes. I rest on the sun lounger. Scents of lavender. I have to put the water on to make tea. From my hands slip the poems of Patti. I keep a bilingual anthology of Rimbaud, in Bilbao. Well, my God, a friend gave it to me as a present, the one who played wolf on my forty-fifth birthday, the same one who got me into trouble. I was so overwhelmed and in a spin, eager to drop, my seams were so poorly stitched, dying to be torn. That's what life was about then, let's say, although the issue is not so simple, not simple at all.

Ladybirds tickle my calves, and I think of water, mouth dry. Hello, gorgeous, he says on arrival. That voice is a knife in the afternoon. Oh Jesus! Have you been unwell, princess, I'll make tea, massage the foot, help take off your sandals, so do not worry, take it easy, my red-haired mermaid. Saliva turns to warm sugar. Unable to open the eyes, so weak I couldn't swallow, beneath the stormy gaze.

The cold teaspoon sends a shiver between my breasts. His long fingers dip in the warm cup, a giggle escapes. Filthy. Now my lips caressed. Knees moistened with sandpaper tongue. Your knees are rum-raisin ice-cream, Meibi, maybe, Meabe, might be. Let's go inside, do not tremble. With the voice, I am ravished. In the jaws of the raider, I am lost.

Cobwebs in the rafters. The planet's leaden clock, bird-bones on the furniture.

Ez naiz beltzarana, ez naiz liraina, ez naiz argia, ez naiz gaztea, ez naiz ahalduna, ez naiz zangarra, ez naiz, ez naiz, ez naiz aingerua, ez naiz deabrua, ez naiz ezer ez bada bizi izan naizena, oroitzen dudana, eta neure izena, izan nahi dudana. Har ezazu buelta, Goikokaleko neska txiki hori, neuk sendatuko zaitut neure esku handiekin.

Marraxoaren bazka ipurmamiak. Egin dzast, dzast, dzast, eder hori, hortxe, eman, segi holantxe, plas, plas, plas. Martiri bat bezala ireki naiz erditik. Tarratada eta bitsa. Izerdiaren perladuria. Zeurea naiz osorik, aleluia. Neurea zara osorik, aleluia, o Jesus!

Bitsa eskuetan (2010)

I am not raven-haired. I am not slim, I am not clever, I am not young, I am not strong, I am not brave, I am not, I am not, I am no angel, I am no devil, I am what I experienced, what I remember, and my name, and what I want to be. Turn around, girl, I will heal you with my great hands.

The buttocks, shark-bait. There, there, pretty, there, my beauty, right there, more, keep it like that, that's it, that's it. I open up like a martyr. Penetration and semen. Beaded and sweating. I am yours entirely, alleluia. You are entirely mine, alleluia, oh Jesus!

Foam in Your Hands (2010)

La Jolie Fille-ren automitologia

Maite ditut parentesiak, masail irriberen antzeko esparru kontrolatuak, etxera apur bat berandu iristea, paisaiaren iodozko kontrasteak.

Maite ditut zehaztasun zalantzagarria, deskribapen inozoak, arrisku baimendua, narritadura eta pixagura eragiten dituzten fosforeszentziak.

Txikitan, urrezko eskumuturreko bat utzi nion neska koxkor bati, berak zabu bat uztearen truke. Etxetik bidali ninduen amak gero, iruzurtiaren bila. Neskatoak ukatu egin zuen gure ituna. Agiraka egin zidatelako gogoratzen dut tratu gaizki egindako hura.

Beste behin —marea bizien sasoian, olatuen kipur horixkak harrapatua baitzuen hondartzaren okotza, zornezko sufle baten antzera—, neska berberak eta haren lagunek biluztu egin ninduten familietan jolasteko, neu nintzela-eta denen panpina. Olatu batek ipurdia busti zidan. Ur lohi hura eta mutiko atzeratu baten begirada gomutan ditudalako gomutatzen dut nire deslaitasuna. Gomutan, halaber, hotza eta lotsa.

Badihardut, beraz, negozio eskasak zenbatzen, kuleroak neuretzat gordetzen, ur nahasiak miatzen, iragana neure alde baliatzearren ezorduan jaikitzen. Otoitz egiten dut inoiz gal ez ditzadan torlojuak doitzeko behar ditudan hatzak.

Zenbat neskato bortxatu dituzte gaur Burundin? Zenbat mutiko hil dira azken minutuan Darfurren? Afganistango haur bat mintzo zait argazki batetik: "Une bat izan nintzen, ez besterik, mosaiko geometriko handian, tesela galkor bat, hain erlatiboa. Gero, dorreen ahoek nire itzala irentsi zuten, eta ez zen ezer gertatu. Amaren ahotsa entzun nuen nire izenaz erditzen, hormako arrakala bat bezala. Gaur egun lasaia da. Nire oinak zaborrontzi batean geratu ziren. Nire bizitza beste alanbrada bat da".

Hona hemen berriz bestelako hotza eta bestelako lotsa. Utz ditzadan bakean babesgabeak. Ez, ni ez naiz inor zuek nik ahotan hartzeko.

Au revoir, la jolie fille, à jamais, la petite, tout est déjà bien vu au temps des adieux. Ça va bien ce soir, hau ez da ezer. Erre ditut koltxoiak eta fakturak, argazkiak, pilulak eta postalak. Ça va bien ce soir, hau ez da ezer, c´est la vie en rose, zoriaren ferra, c´est la vie en rose, anfibioon gerra.

Bitsa eskuetan (2010)

Self-Mythology of La Jolie Fille

I love parentheses, controlled areas like smiling cheeks, arriving home a little bit late, the landscape's violet contrasts.

I love the random truthfulness, faint descriptions, the warranted risk, excitement that produces irritation and the need to pee.

As a child, I paid a small girl a gold bracelet in exchange for a swing. My mother sent me to look for the cheat, who denied our pact. I remember the bad deal only because of the incredible quarrel.

On another occasion—it was a time of spring tides: the cream-yellow of the waves had stained the beach like frothy pus, the same girl and her friends undressed me, to play families. I played everybody's doll. A wave wetted my bottom. I remember my state of neglect, because I remember the dirty water and the look of a retarded boy. I also remember the cold and shame.

For now I have recounted the sorry business, kept to myself the underwear, examined the murky water, I get up at odd times to put the past on my side, I pray never to lose the fingers necessary to tighten the screws.

How many girls are violated today in Burundi? How many died in Darfur this last minute? An Afghan child speaks to me from a photo: "I was only an instant in the great geometric mosaic, one passing tile, that relative. Afterwards, the mouths of towers devoured my shadow, and nothing was done. I heard the voice of my mother giving birth to my name as though a crack in the wall. Today is a tranquil day. My feet remain in the rubbish-tip. My life is more barbed wire."

Here remains a cold and shame of a different order. May the destitute be left in peace. No, I am not worthy to carry you in my voice.

Au revoir, La Jolie Fille, à jamais, la petite, tout est déjà bien vu au temps des adieux. Ça va bien ce soir, This is nothing. I burnt the mattress, and the bills, pictures, pills and postcards. Ça va bien ce soir, this is nothing, c'est la vie en rose, horseshoe luck, c'est la vie en rose, just another amphibious war.

Foam in Your Hands (2010)

Salmoa

parentesi bat da nire gorputza
argibideak onartzen dituena
berrogeita zazpi urteko turmix bat da nire bihotza
kalatxorien moduan miau egiten dut
neure ezpainak haztatzean
part jaurti ditut portura zapata burdinkarak
ez zaitut nahi full time ez zaitut nahi full time
soilik you you you

zure esku handiei begira
zure aho maminari zure oreztei begira
ez du ardura hitzak bai ahotsak
zure bitsak zure gatzak zure esneak
badakizu ez dela merkea armazoiak bazterrean uztea
badakizu azala zirtziltzea dakarrela ortozik ibiltzeak
lasterka nazazu lauhazka lasterkatu lau hankatan
adurra adurraren truke eta adurrean talko-hautsa

iratzezko habia bat egizu biontzat bada toki bat basoan
non basurdearen oinatza non oskilasoaren kanta
non almendrak eta ardo zuria
non zure hatsa eta koadrodun manta
zure besoak txilarrezko bi hego gauzak esplikatzen
zu nire salan zu nire altzoan
zu min zaharrak sakabanatzen
zu zauri berria oinaze sor berriz hornitzen

aintza eta bakea lurrean
kale-kantoia jiratu eta batera
txori bat pausatu baitzait sorbaldan gloria
zure musu bat sorbalda biluzian egunsentian
hain handi eta eder eta on baitzaitut
ardagaia eta su-lama
gloria zu bedeinkatua zu eskerrak zuri ahuspez agur
oi neure erraldoi oi neure masai oi neure irlako moai

Bitsa eskuetan (2010)

Psalm

my body is a parenthesis that accepts clarifications
my forty-seven-year old heart is a blender
ee-i-em-ee-i-em in the manner of a small gull
when I press my lips
I cast my shoes like lead into the port
I do not want you full-time I do not want you full-time
only you you you

looking at your big hands and your mouth
looking at your beauty spot
words do not matter what matters is the voice
your juice, your salt, your milk
you know it is not cheap to park scaffolds on the pavement
you know that walking barefoot wears the skin to a thread
come across to me at a gallop on all fours
breath in exchange for breath and talc in our saliva

build a nest of fern in the woods for two
there the boar's tracks, there the song of the blackbird
there the almonds and there the white wine
there a plaid blanket and there your deep breath
two wings of your arms explaining the heathers
you in my room you on my lap
you spreading the old heart ache
you the fresh wound creating a voiceless sorrow

glory and peace on earth in this way always glory
right after turning the corner of the street
a bird perched blind on my shoulder praise
a kiss of yours on my naked shoulder at dawn
on me on me
you so big and beautiful and good
tinder and flames
praises to you blessed one and thanks to you I bow to you
oh my giant oh my masai oh of my island my moai

Foam in Your Hands (2010)

CASTILLO SUÁREZ

translated by

SUSAN CONNOLLY

Akuarioa

Arrainez gainezka dagoen akuarioari begira ezagutu zintudan. Eskutik heldu nizun eskumuturra hautsita. Marmokak odolusten direnean agertuko nintzela uste zenuen zuk, ordea.

Zer da aurreratzea amore ematea baino. Zer da maitasuna musuan lehertzen den txikle bonba baino.

Elkarri arropa alda diezaiogun, arrainak banan-banan nola hiltzen diren ikusten hasi baino lehen. Bizilagunen autoak leihotik zelatatu baino lehen.

Souvenir (2008)

Aquarium

I met you looking at the aquarium full of fish. I took you by the hand even though my wrist was broken. But you thought I would appear when the jellyfish bleed to death.

Does moving forward not depend upon giving way? Isn't love a chewing gum bubble which bursts on the cheek?

Let's change into each other's clothes—and watch the fish die one by one. Before keeping an eye on the neighbours' cars from the window.

Souvenir (2008)

Panpina mutuak

Jaioko ez diren umeek beldurtzen gaituzte iluntzeetan. Gezurretan hasten gara orduan, hizketa zoroan. Ingurukoen saminaz idazten dugu gurea balitz bezala. Gerria estutzen, birikak lehertu arte.

Ahulak eta tristeak izan nahiko genuke. Bizitza arruntegia dela gurea errepikatu noiznahi eta nonahi. Turismo bidaiak egin besteen beso epeletara.

Negarrak entzuten ditugu trapuzko panpinen ahoetatik.
Panpina mutuak.
Panpinak beti izan dira mutuak.

Souvenir (2008)

Mute Rag Dolls

The unborn babies trouble us at nightfall. That's when we start telling lies, chattering madly. We write about other people's sorrows as if they were our own. We tighten our waists until our lungs burst.

We wish we could become frail and sad. Repeating again and again wherever and whenever that life has become too much the same. To travel like tourists into the warm arms of other people.

We listen to the crying of rag dolls.
Mute rag dolls.
Rag dolls are always mute.

Souvenir (2008)

Beste norbaiten zapatak

Ez dakit beste norbaiten zapatak jantzi dituzun noizbait. Maitale desleial batenak, esate baterako, harengana hurbilduko zintuztelakoan. Ez dakit brikolaje aulki deseroso batean egon zaren bere zain, eta tarteka emakume tristeagoekin larrua jo.

Agian zain zaude petrolio plataforma abandonatu batean, bizilagunen zoriona jasateko gai ez zarelako. Ahaztu dituzu seme-alaben izenak ere.

Gonbidatu lotsatia zara, apika. Ez dakizu dantzan, baina agertokira igoko zinateke eta kantuz hasi, badakizulako heriotzak ez duela inor kantuz harrapatzen.

Beharbada erauzi egin dizkizute hegalak, errautsa jarri betazalen azpian, arkatz hautsiez altxatu ezkatak, edota lixibaz busti ezpainak. Min hori ezaguna zait. Min guztiak dira berdinak.

Souvenir (2008)

Somebody Else's Shoes

I don't know if you have ever worn somebody else's shoes. Perhaps those of a cheating lover, thinking they would bring you closer to her. I don't know if you have sat waiting for her at an uncomfortable work-bench and, in the meantime, you have had sex with unhappier women.

You might be hiding on an abandoned oil rig because you can't stand your cheerful neighbours. You have even forgotten the names of your children.

You might be an awkward guest. You can't dance, but you would go onstage and sing, because you realise—death doesn't come for anyone singing.

Maybe they have ripped out your wings, shovelled ash under your eyelids, lifted up your scales with broken pencils; maybe they have saturated your lips with bleach. I have felt this sorrow deeply. All sorrows are the same.

Souvenir (2008)

Anemonak

Anemonek esnatu zaituzte, inork aditzen ez duen usainak. Belaki-bitsak pozondu zintuen eta kirurgia ebakuntza ikusezin batek ia hiltzen zaitu. Hezurduraraino helarazi zizuten negua eta hasitako guztiak bukatzeko gogo eza. Ahal duzun guztia begiratu dezazun aholkatu dizu medikuak. Zure historia kontatzeko behar dituzun hitzak zureganatu eta maleta gogorretan sartu ditzazun. Galdu daitezen eta munduko edozein aireportutan agertu.

Zurgai (2009)

Anemones

Anemones wake you up, the scent that nobody notices. The foam in the sponges poisoned you and invisible surgery almost killed you. They grafted winter to your bones along with a lethargy which prevents you from finishing anything. The doctor advises you to observe everything. Gather the words you need in order to tell your story and place them in hard suitcases. So that they may go missing and turn up in some other airport.

Wood (2009)

LEIRE BILBAO

translated by

PADDY BUSHE

1977ko urriko gau bat

Urriko gau batez aita eta ama euren logelan,
oraindik ez nire ez beste inoren
aita eta ama ez direnean.

Gizonak jertsea erantzi du:
aulki gainean utziz burua kendu dioten hilotza.
Andreak armairuan sartu ditu galtzak eta alkandora:
pertxatik zintzilik beste emakume urkatu bat.

Bietako batek ere ez dio komodako ispiluari begiratu.
Maindire artera sartu dira
bakoitza bere ohe ertzetik:
mugaren alde biak eta aduana.

Hezetasunak hartutako pareta zatia
irudimenez margotzen ahalegindu da andrea.
Hotzak ditu oinak. Kuzkurtu egin da
gizonaren sabelpera, beroa da haren aho-lurruna.

Argiak itzalita izarak ez dira zuriak;
gorputzak bai, garbiagoak dira.
Andreak eguna du nahiago.
Gizonak gaua.

Urriko gau hartan aita eta ama
oraindik ez nire ez beste inoren
aita eta ama ez direnean
desiratzera behartuta ezkon-ohean
nor bere bazterrean
loak hartzeko zain.

Scanner (2011)

October Night, 1977

An October night and my father and mother in their bedroom,
when as yet they are not
father and mother to anyone.

The man takes off his shirt:
he hangs it on the chair before the mirror, a headless man.
The woman puts her trousers and shirt in the wardrobe:
one more hanged woman suspended on a rack.

Neither of them looks in the mirror on the chest-of-drawers.
They slip between the sheets
each on their own side:
the two sides of the frontier, of customs.

The woman imagines
the damp spot on the wall painted.
Her feet are cold. She takes shelter
around the man's belly, her breath warm.

Lights out, the sheets are not white;
bodies are, they seem cleaner.
The woman would choose daylight.
The man would choose night.

On that October night
when as yet they are not
father and mother to anyone,
in the desire by decree of the marriage-bed
they are waiting for sleep
each one secluding the other.

Scanner (2011)

Terra Nova

> *Nire bizitzan oso goiz izan zen berandu.*
> Marguerite Duras

Berandu jaio zinen
esaten zidan amak.

Bi astez berandutu nintzen
munduari beldurrez.
Beste bi astez izan nintzen
arrain gorri amaren urontzian.

Hiru kilo seiehun
argitu zion irrati-telefonoz aitari.

Ipurdiko bat eta
negar egin nuen aitarentzat.

Nire alaba!
Nire alaba!
entzun zen brankan.
Ondo gabiltza arrantzan
cambio y corto.

Gau hartako marinelen edariak
aitaren kontura izan ziren.
Gau hartan aitak pozik egin zuen lo.

Sei hilabetera ezagutuko zuen
amaren amuko arraina.

Bere besoetan hartu ninduenean
lehen aldiz igeri egin nuen itsasoan.

Badakit ez zela nire negarra
gazitasun busti hura.

Scanner (2011)

Terra Nova

> *Very early in my life, it got too late*
> Marguerite Duras

You were a late arrival
my mother would say to me.

I was two weeks over my time
for fear of the world.
I was a red fish in my mother's womb
two extra weeks in the spawning.

Three point six kilos
she reported by radiophone to my father.

A birth-slap and
I bawled for my father.

My daughter!
My daughter!
echoed at the bow.
Fishing is fine
over and out.

Drinks for the crew that night
were all on my father.
My father slept well that night.

Six months passed before he could meet the shrimp
hanging from my mother's hook.

When he took me in his arms
I swam for the first time in the sea.

Now I realise that it was not only my tears
in all that briny ocean.

Scanner (2011)

Kaleko zakurra

nirea bezain inorena naiz
bere itzala jaten saiatzen den
zakurrari bezala gertatzen zait
urduri jartzen naute maitasun abestiek
badiotsut: irrati dialen zapping-ean
entrenatuta daude nire atzamarrak
orrazi izateari uzten diotenean

berez beleak ditut ilean
batzuetan eskutan hartzen ditut
hegan joaten ez direnean
gertura zakurraren itzala bezala
horregatik galdu nuen aspaldi
galtzearen sentsazioa

mesedez konta iezazkidazu
ahaztu ditzakedan gauzak
poltsa zulatuetatik ihes egiten dutenak
aspaldian pertxak sobratzen zaizkit armairuan
inork ez dit ezkaratzetik
bainugelara dei egiten
aulki hutsez inguratua nago

nirea bezain inorena naiz
kaleko zakurren gisa
itxurak egiten jarrai dezaket
neure buruarekin orain bezala
ohearen beste aldean jarriko naiz adibidez
alde batera begiratzen dudanean
ni baino falta ez nadin

Scanner (2011)

Stray Dog

I am no more my own than anyone else's
stuff happens to me as it happens
to a dog trying to guzzle its own shadow
love songs make me jumpy
I'm telling you: my fingers are trained
from zapping through radio stations
when I stop them from combing

crows nest in my hair
sometimes I hold them in my hands
when they don't leave me
flying close like the shadow of the dog
that is why I lost a long time ago
the feeling of loss

tell me please things I can forget
things that can escape
through a leaking bag
for a long time I have had spare hangers in my wardrobe
nobody calls me from the kitchen
to the bathroom
empty chairs surround me

I am no more my own than anyone else's
in the fashion of stray dogs
I continue to lie to myself
just like at this moment I will
for example move to the far side of the bed
as if I were the one missing
when I look to the other side

Scanner (2011)

Belarra

belarra atera zaio etxeko sofari
egarri naizenean ihintza edaten dut
zerua desertu urdin bat da nire gainean
eta ez dut leiho beharrik
portuak lehortzen doazela ikusteko

farolez eginiko mendi bat daukat aurrean
asfaltoa dut oinetako
olatu beltz estatiko bihurgunez justifikatua

espaloietako losen azpian
aspaldian ez dut izaki bizidunik aurkitzen

gero eta putzu gutxiago daude gure herrian
denbora da ez ditudala oinak uretan busti

belarra atera zaio etxeko sofari
haren gainean luze botata egoteagatik
bueltak ematen ditut nire inguruan
fetuak umetokian bezala neure buruari

zorionekoak
zein mundutan bizi garen zehazki ez dakigunok

Scanner (2011)

Grass

grass has sprouted from the sofa in the house
I drink the dew when I am thirsty
the sky is a blue wasteland above me
and I have no need of windows
to see that harbours are drying up

I have before me a mountain made of streetlamps
asphalt for shoes
a standing black wave edged with bends

it's been a long time since beneath the footpaths
I encountered any living being

all the time there are fewer wells in our village
it's been a long time since I soaked my feet

grass has sprouted from the sofa in the house
from so much stretching out there
I spin myself around
like a fetus in the womb

blessings be upon us
for we do not really know which world we live in

Scanner (2011)

CATALAN POETS

VINYET PANYELLA

translated by

MICHAEL O'LOUGHLIN

AUTORETRAT EN NU

El seu cossi de zenc
aquí és un atuell de plàstic blanc del que em serveixo
als mateixos efectes.
La seva cambra a contrallum, meitat blavosa,
l'altra meitat partida per grocs i rosats càlids,
és aquí d'assèptica fredor:
la que fa el blanc de rajola a la paret
sobre un paviment vermellós dels anys cinquanta.

Després del bany ella ha adreçat el cos desafiant, triomfant,
en èxtasi d'espera.
Les llengües d'humitat em regalimen pels flancs i l'engonal,
fins arribar a la tovallola rebregada als meus peus.
La meitat del mirall li reflecteix un nu pletòric.
Jo em reconec mirant-me els indrets nous de la topografia.
Tot és cos,
matèria capgirada pel somriure sardònic de la carn.
Aquesta línia situa els límits de l'abans i del després
al bell mig del trajecte franquejat pels vials d'artifici
per on s'escolen sang i aigua entre dues bugades.
Horitzó de divisòria d'un mateix territori.

Ell, fora del quadre,
ha resseguit pintant traç i penombra
de la seva acuradíssima toaleta.

Tu no hi ets.
No esguardaràs el nu fendit per la rialla magenta de la carn.

Jo no sóc ella.
La distància que ens separa és la mirada
que va de Pierre Bonnard a Lucien Freud.

Taller Cézanne (2007)

NUDE SELF-PORTRAIT

Here, her tin basin
is a white plastic vessel
I use for the same purpose.
Here, her chamber in *contre-jour*, half blue,
the other half divided by yellows and hot pinks,
has an aseptic chill
coming off the white of the wall tiles
above a red 1950s floor.

After the bath, she has confronted the defiant, triumphant body
in an ecstasy of waiting.
Tongues of damp drip down my flanks and groin
to reach the towel crumpled at my feet.
Half the mirror shows her an abundant nude.
I recognise myself, looking at the new points of topography.
All is body,
matter repudiated by the sardonic grin of the flesh.
This line locates the limits of before and after
right in the middle of the route stamped by vessels of artifice
through which blood and water wash between two laundries.
Dividing line through a single domain.

He, outside the painting,
has traced in paint the line where light and dark meet
in his extremely accurate *toilette*.

You are not there.
You will not regard the nude cut in two
by the magenta guffaw of the flesh.

I am not she.
The distance between us is that of the gaze
from Pierre Bonnard to Lucian Freud.

Cézanne's Studio (2007)

TALLER CÉZANNE

No canviïs de lloc fruites i objectes,
ni el blau polsós de la paret amb les ombres marcades.
El temps va fent la seva.
El que abans era un punt de descurança
ara forma part del decorat.
Tant se val que grinyoli la fusta dels graons.
La tauleta, les teles, el pitxer blau amb flors:
tot és en ordre a l'hora del crepuscle.
Tingues cura que les pomes no es podreixin.
La sentor es barreja amb la volior del jardí.
Fan olor de tu.
    Estima'm.
Procura que no es trenqui. És fràgil
la natura morta de l'amor.

Taller Cézanne (2007)

CÉZANNE'S STUDIO

Don't change the position of objects and fruits,
nor the dusty blue of the wall marked by shadows.
Time will make them its own.
What was a neglected spot
now forms part of the décor.
What matter the whine of the wooden steps?
The table, the cloths, the blue jug with flowers:
at the hour of dawn everything is fine.
Watch out the apples don't rot.
The scent is mixed with the swarm of the garden.
They have your odour.
                            Cherish me.
Don't break it. The still life
of love is fragile.

Cézanne's Studio (2007)

Cerca'm, si vols...

Cerca'm, si vols, en qualsevol terrassa.
Sóc un cul de cafè sense presses ni horaris
quan reposo en un lloc com aquest
aliena a la que era fa una estona.
La identitat?
            I què, si vaig mutant
com l'ombra de les taules i cadires
a cada passa que la llum travessa.
Vine a cercar-me
                     o no, no cal que vinguis.
Sense tu la vida és neutra i sense arestes
que marquin els passatges del dolor
comptat per hores.
No vinguis, no em destorbis,
el café es el norte de los tristes.
M'agrada contemplar qui sóc ben des de fora.
És perillós abocar-se a l'interior.

Aprenent a mirar (2011)

Look for me, if you like...

Look for me, if you like, on some café terrace.
When I'm idling in a place like this
I'm a barfly without haste or schedule
oblivious to what I was a while ago.
Identity...
          And what if I keep changing
as the shadow of the tables and chairs does
with each step the light takes?
Come looking for me,
                    or not, you don't have to.
Without you life is neutral, lacking the edges
which mark the stages of pain
counted out in hours.
Don't come, don't bother me,
the café is the North of the sad.
I like to regard who I am from the outside.
Dangerous to incline towards the interior.

Learning to Look (2011)

Una estona abans…

Una estona abans que tot comenci
m'aixeco amb calma letàrgica i antiga
per mirar-me al mirall i recompondre
la imatge de qui creuen que sóc
perquè no saben que només sóc
en el que escric,
el que escric,
el que omple els quaderns de les ciutats
que m'acullen fortuïtament,
estranyament allunyada de mi,
estrangera que viu dels glops de tinta negra
del que escric
bescanviada amb la lletra de tants somnis.

Sang presa (2011)

A while before...

A while before everything starts
I rise with an ancient and lethargic calm
to look at myself in the mirror and recompose
the image of who they believe I am
because they don't know I only exist
in what I write
what I write,
what fills the notebooks of the cities
which happen to welcome me,
strangely distant from me,
a stranger who lives by sipping the inky wine
of what I write
an exchange with the font of so many dreams.

Bruise (2011)

Vaig viure...

> *No tornis mai als llocs on has estat feliç...*
> Quim Español

Vaig viure perquè tenia un cor de pedra.
S'hi va tornar amb els embats del temps,
travessat per les passions que el van abassegar,
sempre invisibles als ulls dels altres.
Perquè no era el poder dels homes
sinó el de la ment i el del cor
tornats coneixement i amor en un alenar únic,
indivisible com la sang que se'n nodria.
Visc amb el cor arrelat a la pedra
a l'ombra de la vall, a la vora dels arbres,
a prop dels acants, esperant qui sap què:
si un batec d'ales, algun capvespre encès
o el despertar en un jaç de violetes.

Sang presa (2011)

I lived...

> *Never return to the places where you were once happy...*
> Quim Español

I lived because I'd a heart of stone.
Battered by time, it recovered
laced with the passions it hoarded,
always invisible to the eyes of others.
Because it was not the power of men
but that of mind and heart
turned into knowledge and love in a single breath,
indissoluble like the blood which nourished it.
I live with the heart rooted in stone
in the shadow of the valley, at the edge of the trees
near the acanthus, waiting for who knows what:
a wingbeat, a flaming sunset
or waking in a bed of violets.

Bruise (2011)

SUSANNA RAFART

translated by

PAULA MEEHAN

La veu

Salpen els mots cap a crepuscles àrtics,
i el temps és una boira que els retarda.
Digueu-me on sóc, planures atziagues
d'onades frèvoles i vidres breus,
on és el canvi de la veu llaurada
que en terra es lignifica sense arrels?
Amunt, amunt cap al no-res m'inflamo
perquè en la flor extingida sigui encens.

L'ocell a la cendra (2010)

The Voice

Words sail out towards arctic twilight;
time is a fog that slows them down.
Where am I now on these plains of misfortune,
in these choppy waves, these crystal glintings?
Where is the change in my uprooted voice
hardening into wood adrift in earth?
Up, up, I rise towards the void in flames
leaving only the incense of my extinguished flower.

The Bird in the Ashes (2010)

Con tardo vuelo

> *Con tardo vuelo y canto, del oído*
> Sor Juana Inés de la Cruz

Amb vol tardà, damunt les ombres l'ombra
de l'ocell abatut desclosa avança:
sota la llum aprèn la breu condemna
de qui recorda una estremida pau
mentre capçades d'àlbers l'entretenen.
De pedra i foc no n'ha rebut afront,
sola segueix volant a hores petites
com qui destria dolça carn de móres
entre argelagues, runes, dies glaucs,
fins a trobar la branca dibuixada
en el palmell desdit d'un déu mortal.

L'ocell a la cendra (2010)

With Sluggish Flight

> *With sluggish flight and song*
> —Sor Juana Inés de la Cruz

With sluggish flight a shadow falls through shadows,
the bird shot down tumbling towards us.
In the cold light it heard the abrupt death sentence,
carries the memory of that shattered peace
down through the poplar crowns that hinder its fall.
Stone and fire have yet to defile it.
We follow its flight into the small hours
as if searching out the sweetest blackberries
among gorse, overgrown ruins, the hazy days,
until it lands safe on the branching lines
drawn on the ample palm of a mortal god.

The Bird in the Ashes (2010)

En una breu estada

> *Soul, take thy risk*
> Emily Dickinson

Arrisca't, ànima dorment,
hi ha gebre al fang de l'esperança,
cau llum dictada sobre el món.

Al mur obert del teu silenci,
cants muts en heures esberlades
i el mar creixent a boca de fiblada.

Res no obtindràs en la imbatuda calma.

L'ocell a la cendra (2010)

In This Brief Stay

> *Soul, take thy risk*
> *with Death to be*
> *were better than be not*
> *with thee*
>   — Emily Dickinson

Take a chance, sleeping soul:
in the predictable light that falls on the world
frost glints like hope on the mud.

On the open wall of your silence
dumb chants writ between the ivy tendrils,
the sea encroaching with its mouth of hurts.

There is nothing to be had in the face of such calm.

The Bird in the Ashes (2010)

No hi trobareu senyal…

No hi trobareu senyal, però passeu:
endins del marbre esperarà la rosa,
i hi florirà d'amor perquè ho noteu
    sense aixecar la llosa.

La llum constant (unpublished)

You are welcome to enter…

You are welcome to enter though the tomb's unmarked.

There you will find flowering in love

the longed-for rose in deepest dark.

No need to shift the stone that guards the grave.

Steady Light (unpublished)

Què diu l'ocell...

Què diu l'ocell torbat per la tempesta?
Com ha predit l'atzar de font obscura?
No tornarà, no tornarà a la muda
i dolorosa sang del seu casal.

Qui sent humides ales en la nit?
D'on manquen altres vents que no el prevénen?
Res no l'espera, res no el fa avançar:
deixa plomes en l'aire on s'aliena.

Mes, si en trobeu el cos, preserveu l'aigua
que dorm perduda als ulls desarrelats.

La llum constant (unpublished)

What sings the bird…

What sings the bird disturbed by the storm?
When it predicts the fate of the darkest sources?
It won't return. It can't return to the silence,
to the bloody sorrows of its broken nest.

Who hears the beat of drowning wings in the night?
Are there no winds that will save it?
There's nothing to hope for, no reason to go on:
drifting feathers float down through lonely air.

Should you find the body, cherish the reflection
dreaming in its lost, its plucked out eyes.

Steady Light (unpublished)

Senyor, no m'abandonis a l'amor...

Senyor, no m'abandonis a l'amor
la teva llei és forta i se m'emporten,
entre esbarzers, els gossos de la por.
Jo no sé els mals que tants perills comporten.

Senyor, no m'abandonis a l'amor,
amb braços hi aniria fent de barca
vaixell fosc de jacints pel teu enyor
i no em sabria greu al front la marca.

Senyor, no m'abandonis a l'amor:
tinc mans que s'han fet flames de mirall,
no espero de la vida cap licor,
la seva seda no m'és embolcall.

Senyor, no m'abandonis a l'amor,
el cor serà jardí desfet de dàlies
i si és la teva voluntat favor
que esberli en el camí velles sandàlies

dóna'm del tot el vi del meu valor,
que cap aurora no em desperti més,
i siguin els teus ulls primer temor
i sigui el teu silenci el meu decés.

La llum constant (unpublished)

O Lord, do not abandon me to love...

O Lord, do not abandon me to love.
Your rule so fierce, into thickets of thorn
by the hounds of fear I am dragged off,
to danger indifferent, all evils I scorn.

O Lord, do not abandon me to love.
My arms outstretched, the shape of a prow,
a dark ship of hyacinths in the grove,
your brand burned on my willing brow.

O Lord, do not abandon me to love.
Flames in the mirror, these my hands.
I desire nothing from this earthly life.
Stripped of my silks, here before you I stand.

O Lord, do not abandon me to love.
My heart will be a garden of trampled flowers
and, should it be your will, I'll rove
the hard road in worn out shoes forever.

Grant me only the wine to be brave.
Never again let the dawn light wake me,
conquer my fear of your burning gaze.
Let your silence take me.

Steady Light (unpublished)

GEMMA GORGA

translated by

KEITH PAYNE

Llegint Matsuo Bashô

Nit de lluna plena. Els núvols es desplacen
com meduses translúcides pel silenci
impermeable d'aquest aquari fosc.
Som criatures que vivim sota l'aigua
de la tristesa, i per això se'ns fa ardu
eixamplar els pulmons, simplement descansar.
M'atanso a la barana i espero el *plop*
de la granota que es capbussa a l'estany,
els cercles concèntrics que deixen les coses
senzilles quan cauen a profunditat
màxima. Una nit de lluna plena amb Bashô.
I em pregunto: per fer-ne un *haikú* perfecte,
quantes síl·labes li sobren, a la vida?

Instruments òptics (2005)

Reading Matsuo Bashō

Full moon night. Translucent as jellyfish
the clouds move through the impenetrable
silence of this dark aquarium.
We are sad creatures submerged
and find it hard to expand our lungs,
to just rest.
I approach the handrail and await the *plop*
of the frog plunging into the pond,
the concentric circles simplify
what sinks to the depths.
A full moon night with Bashō.
And I ask myself: to make the perfect *haiku*
how many syllables will life spare me?

Optical Instruments (2005)

Quan sona el despertador...

Quan sona el despertador, les primeres a obrir els ulls són les paraules, uns ulls immensos amb els quals déu ens espia. Després s'obren les portes interiors, els passadissos estrets per on avança la llum matinal com un riu d'aigua fresca. L'ordre és lleugerament alterable: ara no podria precisar si s'obren primer els pètals o les campanes, si s'obre primer el meu amor per tu o el teu amor per mi, la dolça sincronia del despertar conjunt. Tot allò que és viu acaba obrint-se, com un pressentiment: les taronges sobre el marbre, el color sobre la matèria, la papallona sobre el perfil, la rosa sobre el coll, el cos sobre el cos. Per què parlar de futur? L'amor no és una línia recta traçada amb llapis sobre el calendari: ni anar, ni arribar, ni avançar. Simplement, obrir-se en cercles delicats, tu la pedra, jo l'aigua.

Llibre dels minuts (2006)

When the alarm goes off...

When the alarm goes off the words are the first to open their eyes, huge eyes with which god spies on us. Then the internal doors open, those narrow passageways through which the morning light flows like a freshwater river. The order could be slightly altered: now I could not say if the petals opened first or the bells pealed, if my love for you opened first or your love for me, the sweet synchronicity of waking together. Everything that is alive is opening, like a premonition: the oranges on the marble, the colour on material, the butterfly in profile, the rose on the neck, the body on the body. Why talk about the future? Love is not a straight line drawn in pencil down the calendar: it doesn't come or go, or advance. It simply opens itself in delicate circles, you the stone, me the water.

The Book of Minutes (2006)

I aleshores ella

Amb farina i aigua treballava
el seu cos. Amb farina i saliva
concebia, inclinava, aprenia
que amb farina i dues mans s'arriba
al dúctil secret de la matèria.
Amb farina i llavis treballava
l'home fins a l'elasticitat
insuportable de la tendresa.
I aleshores lentament tastava
el seu cos, el pa que era el seu cos,
el pa que s'emmotllava tan bé
a les mans com la llum a la terra.

El desordre de les mans (2003)

And Then She

With flour and water she worked
his body. With flour and saliva
she conceived, manoeuvred, learned
that with flour and a pair of hands
comes the yielding secret of matter.
With flour and lips she worked
the man past the unbearable
give of tenderness. And then
she slowly tasted his body,
the bread that was his body,
the bread she had shaped so well
with her hands like light over the earth.

The Confusion of the Hands (2003)

El barquer

Llevar-se d'hora i comprovar que tot és al seu lloc,
que les finestres no han envellit tant en una nit,
que el pa d'ahir segueix tendre per a les dents de llet
del nou dia, que a la cuina perdura l'olor groga
del curri, l'olor de les nostres mans fent el sopar,
fent, lentes, l'amor sota els llençols blancs de la farina,
que els llibres encara conserven, tossuts, la memòria
de les paraules, que tot és, en fi, on ha de ser,
començant pels ossos i acabant per les papallones,
pels meridians i els silencis que ocupen l'exacta
latitud celeste que algú els va assignar. I així, cada
dia, la mateixa feina per passar de l'ahir
a l'avui, per creuar les aigües fosques de la nit
amb èxit i tornar a començar com si res no hagués
passat, tret d'una mica de temps, el fang dels segons.
Fins que una nit embarcarem, però serà un altre
el riu i un altre el barquer. I aleshores, digue'm, ¿qui
mantindrà el nom, qui salvarà l'olor de tot allò
que hem estat, que per nosaltres ha estat, quina mirada
guardarà les finestres, el pa, les mans, la memòria,
els llibres? Quin llot s'atrevirà a engolir tanta vida?

El desordre de les mans (2003)

The Ferryman

Up early to make sure everything is in place,
that the windows haven't aged too much overnight,
that yesterday's bread is still soft for today's milk teeth,
that the golden scent of curry endures in the kitchen,
the lingering aroma of our hands making dinner
as we slowly folded our love through the pastry sheets,
that the books, ah those enduring books, remember all the words,
that everything is, well, just as it should be,
from the bones to the butterflies
across the meridian and the silence that fills the exact
celestial line you've been assigned. Just so, every day,
the same to and fro from day to day,
crossing the dark waters at night just to return
and begin again as if nothing had ever happened,
save for one moment, caught in the mud of seconds.
And one night we will embark, but it will be another river,
another ferryman. And then, tell me, who will keep the name,
who will save the scent of all those things we have been—
that for us has been all—what look will watch the windows,
the bread, our hands, the memory, the books?
What clay would dare swallow so much life?

The Confusion of the Hands (2003)

MIREIA CALAFELL

translated by

THEO DORGAN

Mans que no es toquen…

Mans que no es toquen, pells que no parlen,
i al paladar, el pòsit d'un secret que es desfarà
entre silencis emboirats de tanta melangia
tremolosa pel fred que no vens a combatre
les nits de llençols blancs i finestres tancades.

Ulls que no es besen, versos que cremen
desats al moll de l'ós i del desig
d'un cos que fa de dona en els vestits
de pigues descosides a l'escot
i perfils solitaris que et busquen al coixí.

Escric per a llegir-te. I devorar-te.
Per vèncer la distància que ha imposat l'atzar,
per convertir-te en mot i proposar deliris
amagant-nos del món sota els rellotges
i recitar després els versos
que ens confondran en l'abraçada.

Escric per a escoltar-te. I retenir-te.
Però no hi ets i ja te'n vas.

Poètiques del cos (2006)

Hand not touching hand…

Hand not touching hand; skin not speaking to skin,
and on the palate aftertaste of a secret that melts
among silences clouded with so much melancholy,
trembling because of the cold you are not here to combat,
these nights of blanched sheets, of shut fast windows.

Eyes not kissing eyes, verses that burn
in the marrow of the bone, in the marrow of desire,
a body that presents as a woman in a dress
with unpicked neckline freckles,
lone profile that searches for you on the pillow.

I write that I might read you. And devour you.
To overcome distance that fate has decreed,
to make you into a word, to propose delirium
while we hide from the world under the clocks
reciting the verses
that meld us in a long embrace.

I write that I might hear you, might hold you.
But you are not here, already you have begun to leave.

Poetics of the Body (2006)

TALLS

Potser serà una nit de tempesta
amb trons que exaltaran la pell del cel
i en mostraran les cicatrius
(tallen, les ales dels ocells).
O ni tan sols serà dramàtic
i passarà a les onze d'un dia qualsevol
mentre hi hagi cues per a l'autobús,
nens que desemboliquin l'esmorzar,
i tu estiguis davant de la pantalla
buscant-me en un correu,
amb l'emoció del misteri baixant
dels ulls als dits fins a les tecles
com ocells que picotegen afamats
de gana i de desig. Tant és.
Només importa la consciència del moment,
saber que un dia acabaran
les cues, l'autobús, els nens i els esmorzars.
També nosaltres. El teu nom als meus correus
serà l'últim esbós d'aquesta història,
un crit a l'horitzó tot just abans del vol
(tallen, les ales del present).

Costures (2010)

CUTS

Let it be a night of storm
thunderbolts flashing across the sky skin
the sky showing its scars
(how they slash, the birds' wings).
Or let it be less dramatic,
let it pass before eleven o'clock, an ordinary day,
while people are queueing for the bus, say,
while children unwrap their breakfast rolls,
and you are there before your computer screen,
searching your e-mails for me,
in the grip of a mystery falling
from your eyes to your fingertips,
to the keys at last
like famished birds pecking away,
avid with desire. Let it be.
Only awareness of the moment matters,
to know that a day will come
when queues, bus, children and breakfast rolls will be gone
and we, too, will be gone.
Your name in my e-mails
the last trace of this story,
a cry on the horizon, just before flight
(Ah, how they slash, the wings of the present moment).

Seams (2010)

DIUMENGE

És diumenge des del llit
i no saps quin temps fa a fora
(incògnites que no venien al contracte
d'un segon pis, tercer real, tot interior).

Mandrosa, vas conquerint l'espai
d'un llit de matrimoni que no escau
al complement ni ofereix resistència
i penses què seria llevar-te acompanyada,
l'alegria de fer el mort quasi flotant
en algun somni, sabent que l'escalfor
d'un cos dormint et fa de boia.

Només d'imaginar-t'ho ja somrius
quan l'amenaça de pluja sobta el coixí
i et retreus voler tot el que vols, i dius
escoltant-te la veu, que encara té son:
l'amor romàntic alimenta les putes,
l'amor romàntic alimenta les putes.

Però ni amb la repetició t'has convençut.

Costures (2010)

SUNDAY

It is Sunday. You lie there
not knowing what the weather is like
(a mystery not included in your lease
of this second floor flat that is actually on the third floor
with no view to the street).

Languid and lazy you stretch into the space
of a double bed that fails to match up
to its description, offers no resistance to your claim,
and you wonder how it would be to wake next to someone,
to have the joy of floating there almost adrift
in some dream, knowing that the warmth
of that sleepy body will guide you back.

Just thinking this makes you smile —
and the shadow of rain takes the pillow by surprise;
you reproach yourself for your desires,
you hear yourself say in your half sleep:
romantic love is the food of whores,
romantic love is the food of whores.

You say this over and over, but you do not believe it.

Seams (2010)

PISTES

Sempre s'estima igual però diferent, em deies.
I ara entre el cafè i jo provem d'endevinar
si ens condemnava allò que era igual
o bé la diferència és la culpable.
L'amargor com una pista em porta a tu,
que ets a la cuina i amb la cullera dissols
el sucre que ja no em despertarà.
Del teu gest no es desprèn una resposta,
tan sols l'indici d'una pèrdua. Fixa't:
Jo no tinc ales perquè els omòplats
tornen a ser omòplats si tu no els mires.
I tu que no tens esma per volar.
De tan a prop del terra, ja no caurem.
I estimar és caure.

Costures (2010)

HINTS

All that you love, you love equally but in different ways
you used to say,
and now, between me and the coffee we are trying to guess
if we have been punished by this even-handedness,
or if it's difference that is to blame.
Bitterness, as a hint, brings me to you
there in the kitchen, where you are spooning in
sugar that will not wake me anymore.
There are no answers in your gestures,
only the evidence of loss. Look—
I no longer have wings, my shoulderblades
no more than shoulderblades if you do not look on them.
You have lost the will to fly.
This close to the ground we cannot fall—
and to love, after all, is to fall.

Seams (2010)

Notes

Page 49. 'road movie':
Xohana Torres (1931) is a Galician poet, playwright and novelist. She is a member of the Royal Galician Academy. Torres has been highly influential on subsequent generations of writers, especially on women poets.

Antonio Gamoneda (1931) is a Spanish poet and essayist who has collaborated with painters such as Antoni Tàpies. He has been granted the following prestigious awards: Cervantes Prize, European Prize for Literature, Reina Sofía Award, and National Prize for Literature among others.

Page 51. 'well':
Sargadelos: Galician decorative chinaware which makes use of motifs, forms and colours from Galician folklore.
http://www.sargadelos.com/sargadelos/?txt=grupo&lg=ing

Page 79. '*milia lastur revisited, 1985*':
Itxaro Borda rewrites here an anonymous Basque funeral song from the fifteenth century: *Milia Lasturkoren eresia*. The speakers in these Basque dirges were always women.

Page 129. 'cézanne's studio':
"*at the hour of dawn everything is fine*" [tot és en ordre a l'hora del crepuscle]:
Vinyet Panyella has identified the Catalan poet Joan Vinyoli as the author of this verse.

Page 131. 'Look for me, if you like…':
"the café is the North of the sad" is a variation on a sentence by the Mexican writer Vicente Quirarte from his collection of short stories *Morir todos los días* (2010).

Page 135. 'I lived…':
Quim Español is a Catalan poet and architect. He was awarded the Carles Riba Prize in 1994. He has explored the artistic intersections of architecture, poetry and music.

Page 141. 'With Sluggish Flight':
Sor Juana Inés de la Cruz (1651?-1695) was a Baroque writer from the colonial period, when Mexico was part of the Spanish Empire. When young, she entered the court of the Viceroyalty of New Spain, where she forged a solid literary reputation as a poet, dramatist and scholar. She then became a nun.

Authors and Translators

Juan Arana Cobos is the Etxepare Institute Basque Lecturer at the University of Liverpool. He graduated from the Universidad Autónoma de Madrid with a *licenciatura* in Philosophy. He holds a PhD in Basque Studies from the University of Nevada, Reno, where he was a teaching assistant, research assistant and research scholar. His research interests focus on Basque art and thought, especially on the figure of Basque sculptor Jorge Oteiza. Juan's dissertation 'Jorge Oteiza: Art as Sacrament, Avant-Garde and Magic' is to be published this year by the Center for Basque Studies Press. A further comparative study on the same matter under the title 'Oteiza y Unamuno, dos tragedias epigonales de la modernidad' is also scheduled to be published this year under the auspices of the Foundation and Museum Jorge Oteiza in Navarre, Spain. Juan translated the Basque poems in this anthology into English in order to orient the Irish poets in their versions.

Leire Bilbao Barruetabeña (Ondarroa, 1978) obtained a degree in Business Law from the University of Deusto. She had a successful early start in the field of oral improvisation and then moved on to written literature. She published her first poetry collection, *Ezkatak* [Scales] in 2006 (Susa) and her second, *Scanner*, in 2011 (Susa). A number of her poems have been turned into songs and one of them, 'Irene,' sung by Javier Muguruza, won the Music Prize (Best Basque-language Song) in 2008. Some of her writings have been translated into English, German, Italian, French, Galician, Catalan and Castilian. Her poetry has appeared in anthologies such as *El poder del cuerpo, Desira plazer...*

Bilbao is a regular contributor to various media, participates in individual and collective readings and organizes many different kinds of cultural activities. She has published eight books of children's literature: *Amonak nobioa du, eta zer?* (Elkar, 2006), *Komunean galtzen naiz* (Elkar, 2007), *Markel Gelazikin* (Elkar, 2008), *Martin, egon geldi* (Elkar, 2009), *Garazi Gerezi* (Gero mensajero, 2009), *Teresa Cereza* (Gero mensajero, 2009), *Olagarro bat bainuontzian* (Elkar, 2010), *Armairu barruan ipuinak irakurtzen zituen neska* (Erein, 2010), *Oihana hirian* (Elkar, 2011).

Itxaro Borda (Baiona [Bayonne, France], 1959) began her literary career writing mainly for the journal *Maiatz*, which she co-founded in 1982. Her first collection *Bizitza nola badoan* [So goes life] came out in 1984 in the recently created publishing house Maiatz. She has written poetry, fiction, articles for newspapers, essays and the lyrics of songs for numerous music groups in the Basque Country. In 2002 she received the Euskadi Prize for her novel *100% Basque* and in 2010 the Galician PEN Club Rosalía de Castro Prize.

Her poetry collections include: *Krokodil bat daukat bihotzaren ordez* [I have a crocodile for a heart] (1986), *Just Love* (1987) *Bestaldean* [On the other side]

(1991), *Orain* [Now] (1998) and *Hautsak errautsak bezain* [As much ash as dust] (2002). She has just published in Maiatz a bilingual edition—Basque/French—of the poetry she wrote between 1982 and 2012, with the title *Medearen iratzartzea eta beste poemak/Le réveil de Médée et autres poèmes*.

She is now finishing the fifth novel of her series featuring the detective Amaia Ezpeldoi, in which she deals with the problems of Basque society, its real and imaginary frontiers and its current life from a point of view that could be defined as queer.

She works at the Post Office and is the mother of a 25 year-old daughter.

PADDY BUSHE, born in Dublin in 1948, now lives in Kerry. He writes in both Irish and English, and has published eight collections of poetry, the most recent of which is *My Lord Buddha of Carraig Éanna* (Dedalus, 2012). He has also edited *Voices at the World's Edge: Irish Poets on Skellig Michael* (Dedalus 2010). He has translated the work of a number of contemporary Irish language poets into English, as well as other work from the canon of Gaelic literature. At the moment, he is engaged in translating the work of Sorley MacLean, one of Scotland's most renowned poets, from Scottish into Irish Gaelic. He is a member of Aosdána.

MIREIA CALAFELL (Barcelona, 1980) is a member of the research group "Body and Textuality" at the Universitat Autònoma de Barcelona. She has published *Poètiques del cos* (Galerada, 2006) and *Costures* (Viena Edicions, 2010). She has been awarded the following poetry prizes: Amadeu Oller (2006), the 8th Anna Dodas Memorial (2008) and Josep M. López Picó (2009). Her work has been included in *Noreste. Doce poetas catalanes contemporáneos* (Editorial Espacio Hudson, 2011), *A luz nadadora. 9 poetas recentes de espressão catalã* (Zunái Revista de Poesía & Debates, 2011), *El poder del cuerpo. Antología de poesía femenina contemporánea* (Editorial Castalia, 2009) and *Pedra foguera. Antologia de poesia jove dels Països Catalans* (Edicions Documenta Balear, 2008). Calafell is currently working on the audiovisual poetry reading 'Textures': www.artsmoved.cat/textures

YOLANDA CASTAÑO (Santiago de Compostela, 1977) is a poet, a videomaker, a writer for the periodical press and a very dynamic cultural activist. Since 2009 she has co-directed a series of monthly poetry readings with Galician and international poets for the Municipality of A Coruña and the poetry festival PONTEPOÉTICA in Pontevedra. For five and a half years, she was the co-host of a cultural quiz show for the Galician TV and published three weekly articles in Galician newspapers. She has directed literary workshops and has edited and coordinated collective poetry publications. Castaño has participated in national and international poetry festivals (Portugal, Belgium, USA, Argentina, Peru, Poland, Lithuania, Italy, Slovenia, Nicaragua, Macedonia, Colombia, Ireland, Germany, Venezuela, Austria, Turkey, France, Tunisia, UK, Finland and Japan).

She has been awarded the following prizes: Spanish Critics' 1999, Espiral Maior 2007, El Ojo Crítico 2009 (for the best poetry collection published in Spain by a young writer).

Castaño has published five poetry collections, some bilingual editions (Galician-Castilian) translated by herself, and three books of poetry for children. She is interested in the intersections of poetry with other artistic manifestations such as the plastic arts, music, performance, dance, and the audiovisual industry, which she has explored either solo or in collaboration with other artists, such as for example the interdisciplinary group *Tender a man*. Castaño received a grant to be a resident artist in Villa Waldberta (Munich). Her work has appeared in numerous literary journals in Spain and abroad, in collective books and anthologies (Galician and Spanish) and she has been translated into English, German, Macedonian, Italian, Arabic, Chinese, Armenian, Lithuanian, Japanese, Maltese, Russian, Slovenian and Polish.

SUSAN CONNOLLY was born in Drogheda, Co. Louth. She studied Music and Italian at University College, Dublin. Her first full-length collection *For the Stranger* was published by the Dedalus Press in 1993. Other short collections include her sequence *Boann* in *How High the Moon* (1991), *Race to the Sea* (1999) *Ogham: Ancestors Remembered in Stone* (2000) and *Winterlight* (2002).

She co-authored with Anne-Marie Moroney *Stone and Tree Sheltering Water* (1998), an exploration of sacred and secular wells in Co. Louth.

Susan Connolly was awarded the Patrick and Katherine Kavanagh Fellowship in Poetry in 2001. In the same year she received a Publications Grant from the Heritage Council of Ireland for *A Salmon in the Pool*, a literary and place-name map of the river Boyne from source to sea.

A forty-minute programme about her poetry, *Touched by Winterlight*, was broadcast on ABC National Radio (Australia) in October 2005.

Her poems have been published in journals and magazines throughout Ireland and the U.K. Susan Connolly's second collection *Forest Music* was published by Shearsman Books in 2009. Her poems have been published most recently in *Poetry Ireland Review*, *Shearsman*, and in the anthology *Shine On: Irish Writers for Shine*.

DIANA CULLELL is Lecturer in Hispanic Studies at the University of Liverpool. She holds a PhD in Spanish Literature from the University of Manchester. She specialises in contemporary Catalan and Spanish poetry, and has extensive experience teaching translation at all levels of undergraduate studies. She is currently compiling an anthology of contemporary Spanish poetry for English-speaking students, which will include guided readings and commentaries on the poems. She is also the author of the critical study *La poesía de la experiencia española de finales del siglo XX al XXI* (2010). She has published numerous articles and book contributions on her research specialism, such as 'Versiones postmodernas de compromiso en la poesía española contemporánea: los ejemplos de Luis

García Montero, María Antonia Ortega y Jorge Riechmann' (*Espéculo*, 2009), 'Rewriting *xarneguisme*/ Rewriting cultures: *Xarnego* Poetry and Catalan Identity' (*Journal of Catalan Studies*, 2011), 'Angles morts: la poesía de Àlex Susanna y la creación de lo catalán a través del arte' (*Journal of Iberian and Latin American Research*, 2012), 'Ni príncipes azules ni doncellas: el fenómeno de la reescritura en la poesía de Almudena Guzmán' (*Bulletin of Hispanic Studies,* 2012) and '"Las manos que crean": Esther Zarraluki y la construcción (femenina) de un universo textual a través del tacto' (UAB, 2012). Diana translated into English the Catalan poems by Vinyet Panyella, Susanna Rafart and Mireia Calafell in this anthology in order to orient the Irish poets in their versions.

CELIA DE FRÉINE is a poet, playwright, screenwriter and librettist who writes in Irish and English. She has published five collections of poetry: *Faoi Chabáistí is Ríonacha* (Cló Iar-Chonnachta, 2001), *Fiacha Fola* (Cló Iar-Chonnachta, 2004), *Scarecrows at Newtownards* (Scotus Press, 2005), imram : odyssey (Arlen House, 2010) and *Aibítir Aoise : Alphabet of an Age* (Arlen House, 2011). Her poetry has won many awards including the Patrick Kavanagh Award (1994) and Gradam Litríochta Chló Iar-Chonnachta (2004) and the British Comparative Literature Association Translation Award (1999).

In 2009 Arlen House published a collection of her award-winning plays *Mná Dána*, the same year the Abbey Theatre presented a rehearsed reading of her play *Casadh* which it had commissioned. The film *Marathon*, which she wrote in association with Biju Viswanath, was awarded best screenplay at the New York International Film Festival in 2009. The following year *Rian : Trace*, the short film which she conceived and wrote, received the award for the best international narrative short at the same festival.

Living Opera, in association with *Opera Ireland*, presented a showcase performance in 2009 of the opera *The Earl of Kildare* for which she wrote the libretto. She is currently working on *Lorg Merriman*, three volumes inspired by The Midnight Court.

Further information: www.celiadefreine.com

THEO DORGAN is a poet, prose writer, editor, broadcaster and translator. His most recent collections of poetry are *Greek* (Dedalus Press, Dublin, 2010) and *What This Earth Cost Us* (Dedalus Press, 2008). His translations of the Slovenian poet Barbara Korun were published as *Songs of Earth and Light* (Southword, Cork, 2005), and he was series editor of the European Poetry Translation Network which published, among others, volumes by the Catalan poets Àlex Susanna and Marta Pessarrodona. Dorgan has edited numerous volumes of poetry and essays, and has himself been widely translated—his *Sappho's Daughter* was published in Spanish as *La hija de Safo* (Poesia Hiperión, Madrid, 2001). His prose works deal with the sea: *Sailing for Home* (Penguin Ireland, Dublin 2004) was described by Nobel Laureate Doris Lessing as "a book for everyone", and *Time on the Ocean* (New Island, Dublin 2010) recounts a voyage under sail from Cape Horn to

Cape Town. Theo Dorgan was the recipient of the 2010 O'Shaughnessy Award for Poetry (USA) and is a member of Aosdána, Ireland's academy of the arts.

LUPE GÓMEZ ARTO was born in Fisteus (A Coruña) in 1972. A writer and a journalist, she contributed interviews and essays to the newspaper *Galicia Hoxe* for over ten years. *Pornografía*, her first poetry collection, came out in 1995 and was re-published in 2005 and 2012. Since 1995, she has published: *Os teus dedos na mina braga con regra* (Xerais, 1999), *Poesía fea* (Noitarenga, 2000), *Fisteus era un mundo* (A Nosa Terra, 2001), *Querida Uxía* (Tambre 2002), *Levantar as tetas* (Espiral Maior, 2004), *As bolboretas queren voar* (Concello de Santiago, 2004), *O útero dos cabalos* (Espiral Maior, 2005, Xohán Carballeira Prize, 2003), *Azul e estranxeira* (Edicións do Castro, 2005, Eusebio Lorenzo Baleirón Prize, 2004), *Luz e Lupe* (2005), *Quero bailar* (2006), *Diario dun bar* (Laiovento 2008), *A grafía dos mapas* (Toxosoutos, 2010), and *Diálogos imposíbeis* (Laiovento 2010). Her forthcoming book *O naufraxio das árbores* combines poems and short stories (Laiovento, 2012).

GEMMA GORGA i LÓPEZ (Barcelona, 1968) has a PhD in Hispanic Philology from the University of Barcelona, where she now works as an Associate Professor. Her research has predominantly focused on Medieval and Renaissance literature. As a poet, she has published *Ocellania* (Barcelona, 1997, Rosa Leveroni Prize), *El desordre de les mans* (Lleida, 2003, shortlisted for the Màrius Torres Prize, with a preface by F. Parcerisas), *Instruments òptics* (València, 2005, Gata de Gorgos Prize) and *Llibre dels minuts* (Barcelona, 2006, Miquel de Palol Prize, also in a bilingual edition Catalan/ Spanish: *Libro de los minutos y otros poemas*, València, Edicions de la Guerra, 2009, translated by V. Berenguer and with a preface by M. Sampere). A number of her poems have been translated into Basque, Slovenian, Polish, German, English, French and Italian. She has participated in various readings and poetry festivals both in Catalan-language venues and abroad (Slovenia, Germany, Poland, Venezuela and Chile).

Gorga has also written, in collaboration with Antoni Lozano, an essay on gastronomy entitled *La cuina natural* (Barcelona, 2004, with a preface by N. Comadira).

MAURICE HARMON, a well-known critic, scholar and academic, has written studies of writers from William Carleton to Mary Lavin and Seán O'Faolain, from Austin Clarke and Thomas Kinsella to John F. Deane, Peter Fallon and Dennis O'Driscoll. His pioneering anthology *Irish Poetry After Yeats* appeared in 1978. His reputation as a poet has also grown, particularly with the publication of the acclaimed *When Love Is Not Enough. New and Selected Poems*, 2010, which shows the range and variety of his work. He is also a translator. His *Dialogue of the Ancients of Ireland*, a translation of *Acallam na Senórach*, the medieval compendium of poems and stories, was published in 2009.

ANNE LE MARQUAND HARTIGAN is an award-winning poet, playwright, and painter, and is also a short-fiction and prose writer, actor, director and critic. She has published seven books of poetry and one of prose; the latest poetry collection, *Unsweet Dreams*, in December 2011. Among her many awards she won the Mobil Prize for Play-writing for her play *The Secret Game*. Her plays have been performed at the Dublin Theatre festival, in Beirut, the Edinburgh Festival, Ohio USA, and her play set in Jersey during World War 2, *La Corbière* received critical acclaim and a Fringe First in Washington DC, July 2006. Her award-winning long poem *Now is a Moveable Feast*, published in 1991, will be adapted for theatre. Her paintings and batik have been exhibited in major group shows and one-woman shows in Ireland and abroad. She has six children and lives in Dublin.

KIRSTY HOOPER is Senior Lecturer in Spanish and Galician Studies at the University of Liverpool, specialising in the history of Spain from the 19th century to today. She has particular interests in the networks of people, books and ideas emerging out of contact between Spain and other cultures since 1800, in relational approaches to cultural history, and in the use of digital technologies for humanities research. Her published books include *Contemporary Galician Cultural Studies: Between the Local and the Global* (MLA, 2011; co-edited with Manuel Puga Moruxa); *Writing Galicia into the World: New Cartographies, New Poetics* (Liverpool UP, 2011); *A Stranger in My Own Land: Sofía Casanova (1861-1958), a Spanish Writer in the European fin de siècle* (Vanderbilt UP, 2008); *Reading Iberia: History, Theory, Identity* (Peter Lang, 2007; co-edited with Helena Buffery & Stuart Davis). She is currently working on a digital history project, *Hispanic Liverpool*, and writing two books: a co-authored Cultural History of Modern Spanish Literature for Polity Press, and *The Edwardians and the Making of a Modern Spanish Obsession*. She has translated works from Galician, Spanish and Polish; her Galician translations include Castelao's *Things* and the short story anthology *From the Beginning of the Sea*, both with the Oxford Centre for Galician Studies. In November 2011, she was awarded a Philip Leverhulme Prize by the Leverhulme Trust for her research in Spanish and Galician Studies. She has translated into English the Galician poems by Pilar Pallarés, Lupe Gómez, Yolanda Castaño and María do Cebreiro in this anthology, in order to orient the Irish poets in their versions.

CATHERINE PHIL MACCARTHY's collections include *This Hour of the Tide,* (1994), *the blue globe* (1998), *Suntrap,* (2007), and a novel, *One Room an Everywhere (*2003). Her next collection of poems, *The Invisible Threshold,* is due for publication. Recent anthology publications include *Opening Eyes,* (Cambridge University Press 2009), *Women Poets Writing in English,* (Seren Books 2008), *Field Day Anthology of Irish Literature V* (2002) and *TEXT,* (Celtic Press 2009).

María do Cebreiro Rábade Villar holds a doctoral degree in literary theory. She works as a research fellow at the University of Santiago de Compostela. Her research lines encompass gender studies, poetry studies, and comparatism in the peninsular region, particularly the analysis of literary anthologies as constructive mechanisms of national identity. Her publications include *As antoloxías de poesía en Galicia e Cataluña. Representación poética e ficción lóxica* (2004), *As terceiras mulleres* (2005) and *Fogar impronunciable. Poesía e pantasma* (2011). As a poet, she has published *O estadio do espello* (1998), *(nós, as inadaptadas)* (2002), *Non queres que o poema te coñeza* (2004), *O barrio das chinesas* (2005), *Os Hemisferios* (2006), *Objetos perdidos* (2007), *Cuarto de outono* (2008), *Non son de aquí* (2009) [*I am not from here*, Shearsman Books, 2010], *Poemas históricos* (2010) and *O grupo* (2012).

Miren Agur Meabe was born in Lekeitio (Bizkaia, 1962). A teacher and a Basque philologist, she has worked for the school system and has elaborated school texts in Basque. She is the author of numerous books for young readers. Her first book was a collection of short stories *Uneka... gaba* [At times... at night] published in 1986. She received the Spanish Critics' Prize in 2001 and in 2011 for her poetry collections *Azalaren kodea* [The skin code] and *Bitsa eskuetan* [Foam in your hands] respectively. She has been awarded the Euskadi Prize for children's literature on three occasions for her books *Itsaslabarreko etxea* [The house on the cliff] (2002), *Urtebete itsasargian* [One year at the lighthouse] (2006) and *Errepidea* [The road] (2011). Her album *Mila magnolia-lore* [A thousand magnolium flowers] (2010), in which she combines prose and poetry, has been included in the 2012 IBBY Honour List.

Meabe has participated in literary festivals such as the Dublin Writers Festival (2003), the 8th International Conference of Women Poets (Vitoria-Gasteiz, 2005), the literary festival of Vjlenica (Slovenia, 2006), the Edinburgh Festival (2007), the Instituto Cervantes in Vienna (2008), the Basque Studies Centres of Santa Barbara and Reno (2008), and the Frankfurt Book Fair (2009).

Meabe's work has appeared in collective volumes and anthologies and some of her writings have been translated into other languages such as Braille.

Meabe has been a member of the Basque Language Academy since 2006.

Máighréad Medbh has five published collections and a CD. Born in Co. Limerick, she was a pioneer of performance poetry in Ireland in the nineteen-nineties and continues to impress live audiences with her unique style. Her poetic philosophy is grounded in the integration of mind and body, and she seeks to reflect this in formal structure. The resulting poems range from obviously controlled, carefully planned metres to experimental, random forms in which grammar and syntax are subject to the dictates of mood, sense and music. It is common for Máighréad to sing lines or to chant entire poems. Sense drives vocabulary and form, which in turn direct vocal delivery. Her most recent collection, *Twelve Beds for the Dreamer* (Galway: Arlen House, 2010), reflects her penchant for themed sequences and uses the zodiac as a symbolic framework. In recent years she has written the first book in a planned four-volume story for young readers, a fantasy-fable which is also of large scope, and a book of dialogues and *pensées* on the subject of solitude. The latter will be published by Dedalus Press in 2012. A new edition of her controversial first collection, *The Making of a Pagan*, incorporating eighteen new poems, is also planned for later this year by Arlen House press. Máighréad publishes a monthly blog on her website, www.maighreadmedbh.ie

She lives in Swords, Co. Dublin.

Poet and playwright PAULA MEEHAN was born and raised in the north inner city of Dublin. She studied at Trinity College, Dublin, and at Eastern Washington University in the United States. She has published six collections of poetry; *Dharmakaya* received the Denis Devlin Award and *Painting Rain* was a critical as well as a popular success. She has written plays for both adults and children, including *Cell* and *The Wolf of Winter* and some of her award-winning radio plays were published as *Music for Dogs*. Her work has been translated into many languages with substantial selections of her poetry published in French, German, Japanese, Italian, Polish, Estonian, Greek, and smaller selections published in other languages, including Irish. Some of her poems have been set to music by artists as diverse as Christy Moore, the folksinger, and John W. Brennan, the avant-garde composer. She has been Writer Fellow in Residence at TCD, Poet in Association at UCD, Poet in Residence at DCU and St. Patrick's College, Moderator of the National Writers Workshop hosted at NUI, Galway. She has conducted workshops and master-classes in Ireland, in the UK and in North America. She has also worked with many community groups in her native city, including prisoners, recovering and stabilized drug users, and special interest groups.

MARY O'DONNELL's twelve publications include the poetry collections *Unlegendary Heroes* (Salmon Poetry, 1998), *The Place of Miracles* (New Island, Dublin, 2005) and *The Ark Builders* (Arc Publications, Todmorden, 2009); fiction includes *The Light-Makers* and *Virgin and the Boy* (both from Poolbeg), *The Elysium Testament* (Trident Press, UK 1999) and the short story collection *Storm Over Belfast* (New Island, 2008). She is co-editor with Manuela Palacios of the anthology of Galician women's poetry, *To the Winds Our Sails* (Salmon Poetry, 2010). She teaches creative writing in NUI Maynooth's Department of English and is a member of Aosdána. In spring 2012 she was an artist in residence at the Irish College in Paris. www.maryodonnell.com

MICHAEL O'LOUGHLIN was born in Dublin in 1958, and educated at Trinity College Dublin. From 1980 to 2002 he lived mainly in Spain and the Netherlands, but now lives in Dublin. He has published five collections of poetry, the most recent of which is *In This Life* (New Island, 2011). In addition, he has written critical essays, short stories, and screenplays for feature films, including *Snapshots* (2003). He is also active as a translator and has translated more than one hundred books from the Dutch. He has been Writer in Residence for Galway City and County, and Writer Fellow in the School of English, Trinity College. He has been the recipient of many awards and grants, most recently the Patrick and Katherine Kavanagh Fellowship.

PILAR PALLARÉS (Culleredo, A Coruña, 1957) is a poet, essayist and literary critic, and has taught Galician literature in the secondary-school system. She was already a prominent writer in the 1980s and obtained the Esquío Poetry Prize in 1983. Her poetry collections include: *Entre lusco e fusco* (1980), *Sétima soidade* (1984), *Livro das devoracións* (1996), which obtained the Spanish Critics' Prize, and *Leopardo son* (2011). Among her literary studies, we could mention: *Rosalía: unha leitura feminista* (1985), *Rosas na sombra (A poesía de Luís Pimentel)* (1991) and, together with Laura Tato, *Ricardo Carvahlo Calero: a dignidade persoal* (1994) and *Rafael Dieste* (1995). Pallarés has participated in collective publications such as *De amor e desamor* (1984 and 1985) and her work has appeared in important anthologies of contemporary poetry. She has been a regular contributor to literary journals and newspapers.

VINYET PANYELLA (Sitges, Catalunya/Spain) is a writer, a poet, a cultural manager and a curator of art exhibitions. She is the author of numerous essays on art, literature and modern cultural history. Panyella was the Manager of the Catalunya Library (1989-2006) and its Director (2000-2004). Since December 2011, she has been the Director of the Sitges museums (Consorci del Patrimoni de Sitges). She has been publishing a blog and a web page *Quadern de Terramar* (www.quaderndeterramar.wordpress.com) since 2006.

Panyella is the author of fourteen poetry collections: *Memorial de platges* Rosa Leveroni Poetry Prize (1993), *Les ales del buit* (1997), *Jardí d'ambre*, Recull Poetry Prize (1998), *Miralls de marbre*, with drawings by J.M.Subirachs (2000), *Quintet de L'Havana (Un homenatge a Alejo Carpentier)* (2001), *París-Viena* (2002), *Written for the Darkness. An Anthology* (2004), *Dins del cercle d'Orfeu* (2004), *Taller Cézanne* (2007), Màrius Sampere International Poetry Prize, 2006, *Exposició antològica* (2008), *Cavalls i collaret. Suite de Terramar*, trilingual edition Catalan/Castilian/English (2009), *Aprenent a mirar*, with photographs by Quim Curbet (2011), *Sang presa*, Miquel de Palol de Poesia Poetry Prize, 2011, *La mar que se m'enduu* (Suite Camille Claudel) (2012).

Panyella's poetry has been included in anthologies such as: *Paisatge emergent. Trenta poetes catalanes del segle XX* (1999), *Antologia de poetes d'expressió catalana*, by Helena Zernova (Sant Petersburg, 2001), *Antologia de poesia catalana femenina*, Coord. Carme Riera (2003), *Poetes òrfics catalans*, Coord. Francesc Ruiz Soriano

(2007), *De tweede ronde. Catalonië-nummer* (Amsterdam, 2008). She has translated René Char's *Les voisinages de Van Gogh/ Els veïnatges de Van Gogh* (2003), poems by Albert Camus, Marguerite Yourcenar, Umberto Saba, as well as both poems and prose by Marina Tsvetàieva. She has published the anthology of women poets *Contemporànies. Antologia de poetes dels Països Catalans* (1999). Her poetic theory is expounded in 'El dard i el poema' *(Els Fulls de l'Escriptori 2011)*. Panyella is a founding member of the poetry journal *Poetari* (2012). Her poetry has been translated into Castilian, Portuguese, Maltese, English, Russian, Croatian and Dutch.

CHUS PATO (Galicia, 1955) has published the following collections of poetry: *Urania* (Ourense, Calpurnia, 1991), *Heloísa* (A Coruña, Espiral Maior, 1994), *Fascinio* (Muros, Toxosoutos, 1995), *Nínive* (Vigo, Edicións Xerais, 1996), *A ponte das poldras* (Santiago de Compostela, Noitarenga, 1996; 2nd. ed.: Vigo, Galaxia, 2006), *m-Talá* (Vigo, Edicións Xerais, 2000), *Charenton* (Vigo, Edicións Xerais, 2003), *Hordas de escritura* (Vigo, Edicións Xerais, 2008), *Secesión* (Vigo, Galaxia, 2009) and the anthology with readings of her poetry *Nacer é unha república de árbores* (Cumio. Pontevedra, 2011).

Erín Moure has translated three of her collections into English: *From m-Talá* (Vancouver: Nomados, 2003), *Charenton* (Exeter and Ottawa: Shearsman Books & BuschekBooks, 2007), *m-Talá* (Shearsman Books & BuschekBooks, 2009) and *Hordes of writing* (Shearsman Books & BuschekBooks, 2011).

A number of Chus Pato's collections have also been translated into Castilian and many of her poems have been translated to other languages and have been published in prestigious anthologies such as: *New European Poets, ed.* Wayne Miller and Kevin Prufer (Saint Paul, MN: Graywolf Press, 2008); *20 Canadian Poets Take on the World*, edited by Priscila Uppal (Toronto, ON: Exile Editions, 2009); *To the Winds Our Sails; Irish Writers Translate Galician Poetry*, eds. Mary O'Donnell and Manuela Palacios (Cliffs of Moher: Salmon Poetry, 2010) and *Contemporany Galician Poets (A Poetry Review Supplement)*, selected and translated by Jonathan Dunne (London, 2010).

Nínive was awarded the Losada Diéguez Prize and *Hordas de escritura* was granted both the Spanish Critics' Prize and the Losada Diéguez Prize.

In 2012 she was invited to participate in the international poetry festival in Rotterdam.

KEITH PAYNE is an Irish writer currently living in Salamanca, Spain. His poetry has been performed and published in Sydney, New York, Ireland and Spain, places where he has lived over the past decade. Most recently, translations of Catalan author Víctor Balcells have appeared in Ireland. Forthcoming translation projects include the stage-work , *The Dilemmas of Professor Heyman* by Nicolás Paz Alcalde. Keith teaches English literature at the University of Salamanca and continues translating Hispanic authors while assembling a first collection of poetry. Keith can be contacted at keith.payne@mac.com

SUSANNA RAFART (Ripoll, 1962) is a Professor of Spanish Language and Literature in the secondary school system. She has written criticism, essays and poetry translations for various journals and participates in the *Poetary* journal project. She was awarded the Carles Riba Prize in 2001 for her poetry collection *Pou de glaç* (2002). Other poetry books she has published are: *Olis sobre paper* (1996) Senyoriu d'Ausiàs March Prize, *A cor què vols* (1997). *Reflexió de la llum* (1999) Joan Teixidor Prize, *Jardins d'amor advers* (2000), Joan Alcover Prize, *Retrat en blanc* (2004), *Molí encès /Molino en llamas* (2005) *Baies* (2005) *L'ocell a la cendra* (2010), *La mà interior* (2011). Her prose work related to poetry includes: *Un cor grec. Memòria i notes d'un viatge* (2006), *Gaspara Stampa. Sobre l'amor. Retrat oval de Gaspara Stampa amb intervencions presents* (2011), *Els xiprers tentaculars. Una aproximació al paisatge de Maria Àngels Anglada* (2011). Rafart has also published fiction: *La pols de l'argument* (2000) *La inundació* (2003, Serra d'Or Critics' Prize, 2004), *Les tombes blanques. Contes de la Mediterrània* (2008) Qwerty BTV Prize. Her books for children include: *Els gira-sols blaus* (1993), *Pirata 101* (1995), *El viatge de Kira i Jan*, a children's cantata in collaboration with the musician Salvador Brotons (2002). Rafart has translated work by Dino Campana, Leonardo da Vinci, Salvatore Quasimodo and Yves Bonnefoy.

LORNA SHAUGHNESSY was born in Belfast and lives in Co Galway, where she lectures in Spanish in the National University of Ireland, Galway. She has published two collections of poems, *Torching the Brown River* (Salmon Poetry 2008) and *Witness Trees* (Salmon Poetry 2011). She has translated contemporary Mexican poets María Baranda and Pura López-Colomé (Arlen House, 2006) and Galician poet Manuel Rivas (Shearsman Books, 2012). She also contributed to *To the Winds Our Sails*, an anthology of Galician women poets (Salmon Poetry, 2010).

CASTILLO SUÁREZ (Alsasua, 1976) works for the local administration as a Basque-language specialist. She is also a regular contributor to various Basque-language media. Suárez has already published several collections of poetry: *Amodio galduak* [Lost loves] (Ayuntamiento de Pamplona 1999), *Bitaminak* [Vitamines] (Ayuntamiento de Pamplona 2000), *Iragarki merkeak* [Business advertisements] (Diputación Foral de Álava 2000), *Madarikazioa* [Malediction] (Diputación Foral de Álava 2003), *Mugarri estaliak* [Concealed limits] (Susa 2000), *Spam poemak* [Spam poems](Elkar 2004), *Bala hutsak* [Hollow bullets] (Elkar 2006) and *Souvenir* (2008). Of late, she has focused on children's literature and has published several books in this genre: *Ebelina Mandarina* (Erein 2010), *Nobio bat nire amarentzat* [A boyfriend for my mother] (Elkar 2011) *Muxurik nahi?/¿Te doy un beso?* (Mezulari 2011) and *Krispeta hegalariak* [Flying pop-corn] (Elkar 2012).

About the Editor

Manuela Palacios is Associate Professor of English Literature at the University of Santiago de Compostela in Spain. She has directed several research projects on contemporary Irish and Galician women writers, which have been funded by the Spanish Ministry of Science and Innovation. She has co-edited three books on this topic: *Palabras extremas* (with Helena González; Netbiblo 2008), *Writing Bonds* (with Laura Lojo; Peter Lang 2009), *Creation, Publishing, and Criticism* (with María Xesús Nogueira and Laura Lojo; Peter Lang, 2010). Palacios has also co-edited with Mary O'Donnell the anthology *To the Winds Our Sails. Irish Writers Translate Galician Poetry* and she edited and co-translated with Arturo Casas the bilingual anthology of Irish women poets *Pluriversos* (Follas Novas 2003). Her other publications include translations of European poetry and Virginia Woolf's fiction into Galician, as well as monographs on Virginia Woolf's pictorial imagery and William Shakespeare's *Richard III*.

Sources and Permissions
for previously-published poems

Galician Poets

Pilar Pallarés, *Libro das devoracións*. A Coruña: Espiral Maior, 1996. Spanish Critics' Prize, 1996.
Pilar Pallarés, *Leopardo son*. A Coruña: Espiral Maior, 2011.
Chus Pato, *O ritmo do ollo*. Unpublished.
Lupe Gómez Arto, *Pornografía*. Vigo: Writer's edition, 1995. Santiago de Compostela: Editorial Compostela, 2005. Santiago de Compostela: Edicións Positivas, 2012.
Lupe Gómez Arto, *Diálogos imposíbeis*. Ames: Laiovento, 2010.
Yolanda Castaño, 'Pero eu, filla das miñas fillas…' in *Yo es otro. Autorretratos de la nueva poesía*. Coord. Josep M. Rodríguez. Barcelona: DVD Ediciones, 2001.
Yolanda Castaño, *Profundidade de campo*. A Coruña: Espiral Maior, 2007. Espiral Maior Prize, 2007. Bilingual edition with Spanish translation: *Profundidad de campo*. Barcelona: Visor, 2009. El Ojo Crítico Prize, 2009.
María do Cebreiro, *Os hemisferios*. Vigo: Galaxia, 2006.
María do Cebreiro, 'Eran follas pequechas…' Unpublished.
María do Cebreiro, *Poemas históricos*. Writer's edition in collaboration with X. Carlos Hidalgo. Santiago de Compostela, 2010.

Basque Poets

Itxaro Borda, *Krokodil bat daukat bihotzaren ordez*. Zarautz: Susa, 1986.
Itxaro Borda, 'Be My Woman,' 'Kartz,' 'Maria Merceren (B)Egia,' 'Outside.' Unpublished.
Miren Agur Meabe, *Bitsa eskuetan*. Zarautz: Susa, 2010. Spanish Critics' Prize, 2011.
Castillo Suárez, *Souvenir*. Donostia: Elkar, 2008.
Castillo Suárez, 'Anemonak' in *Zurgai*, July 2009: 103.
Leire Bilbao, *Scanner*. Zarautz: Susa, 2011.

Catalan Poets

Vinyet Panyella, *Taller Cézanne*. Santa Coloma de Gramenet: La Garúa Libros, 2007.
Vinyet Panyella, *Aprenent a mirar*. Girona: Curbet Edicions, 2011.

Vinyet Panyella, 'Una estona abans que tot comenci,' 'Vaig viure perquè tenia un cor de pedra.' *Sang presa*. Miquel de Palol Prize, 2011. Barcelona: Columna, 2011. Licence granted by Columna Edicions Llibres i Comunicació, S.A.U., Columna. Vinyet Panyella © 2011.

Susanna Rafart, *L'ocell a la cendra*. Cornellà de Llobregat: Alabatre / Edicions LaBreu, 2010.

Susanna Rafart, 'No hi trobareu senyal, però passeu,' 'Què diu l'ocell torbat per la tempesta?,' 'Senyor, no m'abandonis a l'amor.' Unpublished.

Gemma Gorga, *El desordre de les mans*. Lleida: Pagès Editors, 2003. 2nd. ed. 2008.

Gemma Gorga, *Instruments òptics*. València: Brosquil, 2005. Gorgos Prize, 2004.

Gemma Gorga, 'Quan sona el despertador…'. *Llibre dels minuts*. Barcelona: Columna, 2006. Licence granted by Columna Edicions Llibres i Comunicació, S.A.U., Columna. Gemma Gorga © 2006. Miquel de Palol Prize, 2006.

Mireia Calafell. *Costures*. Barcelona: Viena, 2010. Josep López Picó Prize, 2009.

Mireia Calafell. *Poètiques del cos*. Cabrera de Mar: Galerada, 2006. Amadeu Oller Prize, 2006.

www.ingramcontent.com/pod-product-compliance
Lightning Source LLC
Chambersburg PA
CBHW022010160426
43197CB00007B/370